B E R N A R D   T S C H U M I
C I N E G R A M   F O L I E
L E P A R C D E L A V I L L E T T E

"In madness equilibrium is established, but it masks that equilibrium beneath the cloud of illusion, beneath feigned disorder; the rigor of the architecture is concealed beneath the cunning arrangement of the disordered violences."—Michel Foucault, Madness and Civilization.

"Cinegram: not a fixed, unique or even repeated object; but a combination (of objects or spaces) • A notation of images and movements • Writing in movement • Discontinuous continuous."

"Madness would then be a word in perpetual discordance with itself and interrogative throughout, so that it would question its own possibility, and therefore the possibility of the language that would contain it; thus it would question language itself, since the latter also belongs to the game of language."—Maurice Blanchot

"The world for us, has become infinite, meaning that we cannot refuse it the possibility to lend itself to an infinity of interpretations."—Nietszche, Le Gai Savoir

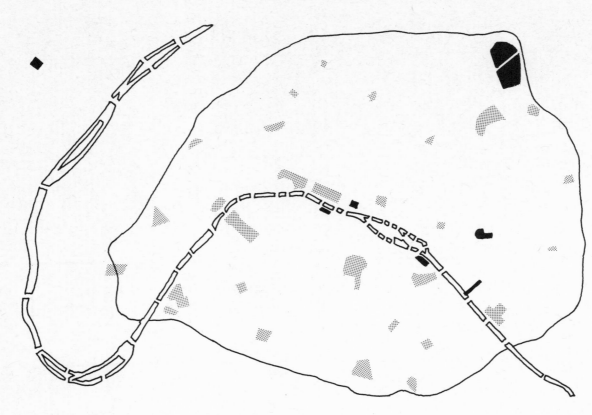

PLAN OF PARIS WITH SITES OF "GRANDS PROJETS" AND EXISTING PARKS

P R E F A C E

The competition for the Parc de la Villette was organized by the French Government in 1982. Its objectives were both to mark the vision of an era and to act upon the future economic and cultural development of a key area in Paris. As with other "Grands Projets," such as the Opera at Bastille, the Louvre Pyramid or the Arch at Tête-Défense, the Parc de la Villette was the center of numerous polemics, first at the time of the competition, when landscape designers violently opposed the challenges of architects, then during governmental changes and various general budgetary crises.

The Parc de la Villette is located on one of the last remaining large sites in Paris, a 125-acre expanse previously occupied by the central slaughter houses and situated on the Northeast corner of the City, between the Metro stations Porte de Pantin and Porte de la Villette. Over one kilometer long in one direction and seven hundred meters in the other, La Villette appears as a multiple programmatic field, containing, in addition to the park, a large Museum of Science and Industry, a City of Music, a Grande Halle for exhibitions, and a rock concert hall.

Despite its name, the park as designated in the competition was to be no simple landscape replica. On the contrary, the brief for this "Urban Park for the 21st Century" develops a complex program of cultural and entertainment facilities encompassing open air theaters, restaurants, art galleries, music and painting workshops, playgrounds, video and computer displays, as well as the obligatory gardens where cultural invention rather than natural re-creation, was encouraged. The object of the competition was to select a chief architect who would oversee the masterplan and also build the "structuring" elements of the park. Artists, landscape designers and other architects were to contribute a variety of gardens or buildings.

In March 1983, Bernard Tschumi, a 39-year old French-Swiss architect living in New York, was selected by an international jury from over 470 teams from 70 countries. His winning scheme had been conceived as a large metropolitan venture, derived from the disjunctions and dissociations of our time. It attempted to propose a new urbanistic strategy by articulating concepts such as "superimposition," architectural "combination" and "cinematic" landscapes. Tschumi described the Park as "the largest discontinuous building in the world."

Tschumi is currently completing the $130 million first phase of La Villette. As of late 1987, nearly half of the Park is under construction, including 15 of 35 *Folies*, part of the covered galleries, the bridge and segments of the "cinematic promenade" of gardens. Several gardens by individual designers are under way, while future building projects are under consideration.

This book assembles in one volume a few key documents from the nearly 4,000 drawings and 70 models elaborated over the past three years. It also presents a theoretical introduction and several texts written during the development stages of the project, including extracts from the competition report, the feasibility study, and project descriptions.

✓ Another book by Bernard Tschumi, *La Case Vide*, (Folio VIII, Architectural Association, 1986), expands the Park's concept beyond its built phase and includes a major essay "Point de Folie. Maintenant l'Architecture," by Jacques Derrida, as well as a contribution by Anthony Vidler and an interview by Alvin Boyarsky.

✓ Also, a publication entitled *Parc-Ville Villette*, (Ed. Champ Vallon, 1987), illustrates contributions of the artists, landscape designers, architects and philosophers.

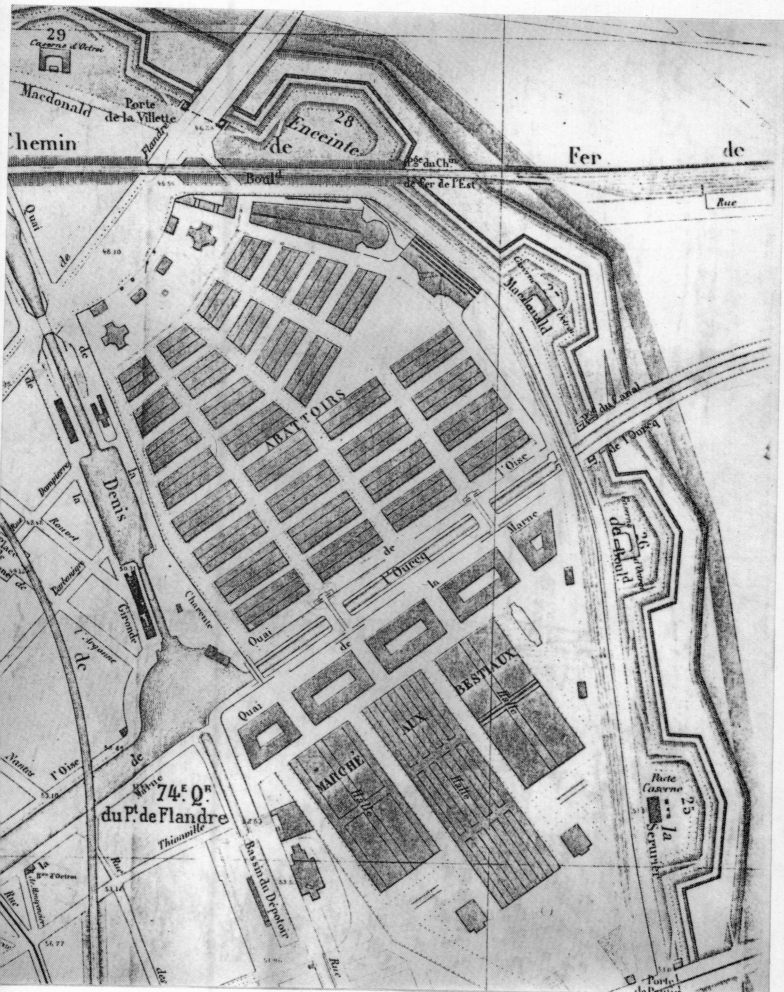

THE SLAUGHTERHOUSES AT LA VILLETTE, PLAN, 1865

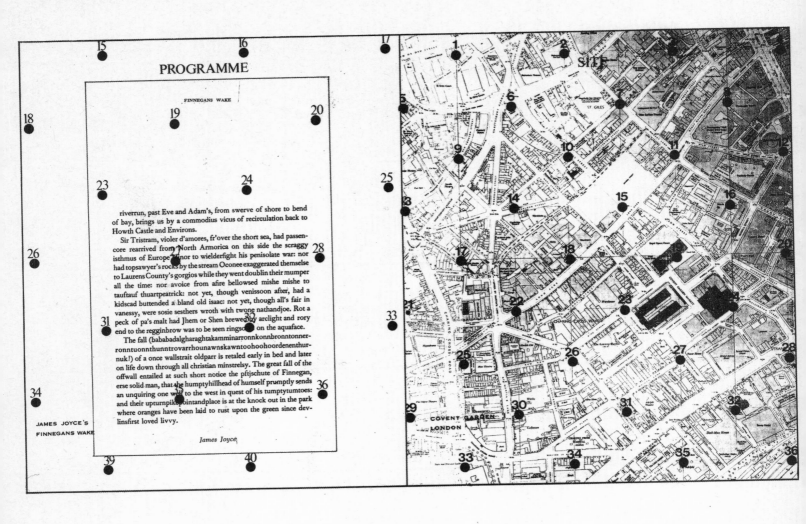

ABSTRACT MEDIATION AND STRATEGY

When confronted with an urbanistic program, an architect may either:

a) design a masterly construction, an inspired architectural gesture (a composition);

b) take what exists, fill in the gaps, complete the text, scribble in the margins (a complement);

c) deconstruct what exists by critically analyzing the historical layers that preceded it, even adding other layers derived from elsewhere—from other cities, other parks (a palimpsest);

d) search for an intermediary—an abstract system to mediate between the site (as well as all given constraints) and some other concept, beyond city or program (a mediation).

During the Parc de la Villette competition, thought had been given to employing as a methodology either the palimpsest or the abstract mediation. The composition and complement were rejected outright, the one for its subscription to old architectural myths, the other for its limiting pragmatism. Yet the palimpsest (which had been explored in the 1976 *Screenplays*) was not pursued, for its inevitably figurative or representational components were incompatible with the complexity of the programmatic, technical and political constraints that could be foreseen. Furthermore, the object of the competition was both to select a chief architect who would be in charge of the master plan as well as of construction of the park's key elements, and to suggest, coordinate and supervise possible contributions by other artists, landscape designers and architects. The numerous unknowns governing the general economic and ideological context suggested that much of the chief architect's role would depend on a strategy of substitution. It was clear that the elements of the program were interchangeable and that budgets and priorities could be altered, even reversed, at least over the course of one generation.

Hence the concern reinforced by recent developments in philosophy, art and literature, that the park propose a strong conceptual framework while simultaneously suggesting multiple combinations and substitutions. One part could replace another, or a building's program be revised, changing (to use an actual example) from restaurant to gardening center to arts workshop. In this manner, the park's identity could be maintained, while the circumstantial logics of state or institutional politics could pursue their own independent scenarii. Moreover, our objective was also to act upon a strategy of differences: if other designers were to intervene, their projects' difference from the *Folies* or divergence from the continuity of the cinematic promenade would become the condition of their contributions. The general circumstances of the project, then, were to find an organizing structure that could exist independent of use, a structure without center or hierarchy, a structure that would negate the simplistic assumption of a causal relationship between a program and the resulting architecture.

Recourse to the point grid as an organizing structure was hardly without precedent. The concept of an abstract mediation had been researched earlier in *Joyce's Garden* (1977), in which a

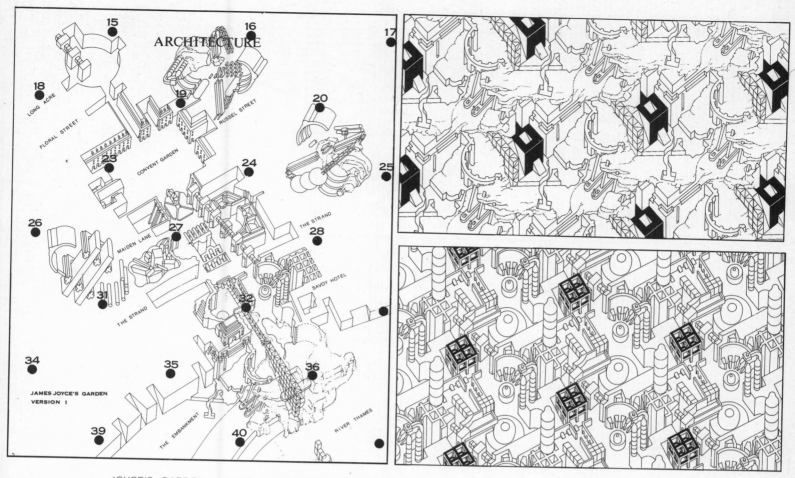

JOYCE'S GARDEN 1976-77: A LITERARY TEXT, *FINNEGANS WAKE*, WAS USED AS THE PROGRAM. AN ABSTRACT POINT GRID FUNCTIONED AS A MEDIATOR BETWEEN THE TEXT AND THE SITE

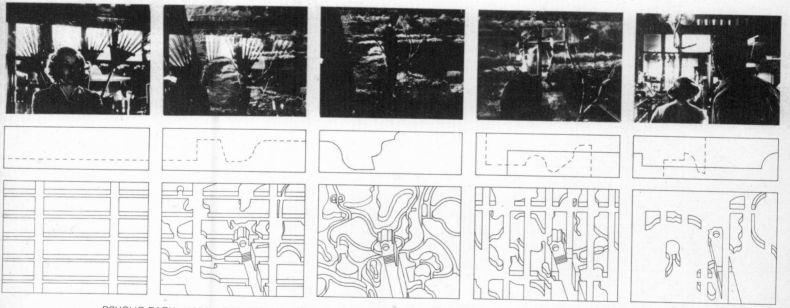

PSYCHO-PARK (1976), EXCERPT FROM THE *SCREENPLAYS* SERIES: FADE-IN, FADE-OUT AS PALIMPSEST: SUPERIMPOSITION OF ABSTRACT AND FIGURATIVE ELEMENTS EDITED FROM A. HITCHCOCK'S *PSYCHO* AND PLANS FROM CENTRAL PARK AND MANHATTAN GRID

literary text, *Finnegans Wake*, was used as the program for a project involving a dozen contributions by different students on a ''real'' site, London's Covent Garden. The intersections of an ordinance survey grid became the locations of each architectural intervention, thereby accomodating a heterogeneous selection of buildings through the regular spacing of points. Moreover (and perhaps more importantly) the point grid functioned as a mediator between two mutually exclusive systems of words and stones, between the literary program (Joyce's book) and the architectural text. *Joyce's Garden* in no way attempted to reconcile the disparities resulting from the superimposition of one text on another; it avoided synthesis, encouraging, instead, the opposed and often conflicting logics of the different systems. Indeed, the abstraction of the grid as an organizing device suggested the disjunction between an architectural signifier and its programmatic signified, between space and the use that is made of it. The point grid became the tool of an approach that argued, against functionalist doctrines, that there is no cause-and-effect relationship between the two terms of program and architecture.

Beyond such personal precedents, the point grid was also one of the few modes of spatial organization that vigorously resisted the stamp of the individual author: its historical multiplicity made it a sign without origin, an image without "first image" or inaugurating mark. Nevertheless, the grid's serial repetitions and seeming anonymity made it a paradigmatic 20th-century form. And, just as it resisted the humanist claim to authorship, so it opposed the closure of ideal compositions and geometric dispositions. Through its regular and repetitive markings, the grid defined a potentially infinite field of points of intensity: an incomplete, infinite extension, lacking center or hierarchy.

The grid, then, presented the project team with a series of dynamic oppositions. We had to design a park: the grid was anti-nature. We had to fulfill a number of functions: the grid was anti-functional. We had to be realists: the grid was abstract. We had to respect the local context: the grid was anti-contextual. We had to be sensitive to site boundaries: the grid was infinite. We had to take into account political and economic indetermination: the grid was determinate. We had to acknowledge garden precedents: the grid had no origin, it opened onto an endless recession into prior images and earlier signs.

S U P E R I M P O S I T I O N

It should be noted that the point grid of La Villette could just as well have taken the form of a random distribution of points throughout the site. Only for strategic, rather than conceptual, reasons was the regular point grid selected. It is also important to recall that the point grid of *Folies* (the "system of points") constitutes only one of the project's components; the "system of lines" and the "system of surfaces" are as fundamental as the "system of points."

Each represents a different and autonomous system (a text), whose superimposition on another makes impossible any "composition," maintaining differences and refusing ascendency of any privileged system or organizing element. Although each is determined by the architect as "subject," when one system is superimposed on another, the subject—the architect—is erased. While one could object that the same architect continues his controlling authority by staging the superimposition (and hence that the park remains the product of his individual intentions), the competition requirements provided a means to relativize the presence of such a masterminding subject by stipulating, as in any large-scale urban project, that other professionals intervene. Another layer, another system could then be interposed among the preceding three layers in the form of occasional constructions juxtaposed to several *Folies*, or of experimental gardens by different designers, inserted into the sequences of the cinematic promenade. Such juxtapositions would be successful only insofar as they injected discordant notes into the system, hence reinforcing a specific aspect of the Park theory. The principle of heterogeneity—of multiple, dissociated and inherently confrontational elements—is aimed at disrupting the smooth coherence and reassuring stability of composition, promoting instability and programmatic madness ("a Folie"). Other existing constructions (e.g. the Museum of Science and Industry, the Grande Halle) add further to the calculated discontinuity.

C I N E G R A M

To the notion of composition, which implies a reading of urbanism on the basis of the *plan*, the La Villette project substitutes an idea comparable to montage (which presupposes autonomous parts or fragments). Film analogies are convenient, since the world of the cinema was the first to introduce discontinuity—a segmented world in which each fragment maintains its own independence, thereby permitting a multiplicity of combinations. In film, each frame (or photogram) is placed in continuous movement. Inscribing movement through the rapid succession of photograms constitutes the cinegram.

The Park is a series of cinegrams, each of which is based on a precise set of architectonic, spatial or programmatic transformations. Contiguity and superimposition of cinegrams are two aspects of montage. Montage, as a technique, includes such other devices as repetition, inversion, substitution and insertion. These devices suggest an art of rupture, whereby invention resides in contrast—even in contradiction.

D E C O N S T R U C T I O N

Is the Parc de la Villette a built theory or a theoretical building? Can the pragmatism of building practice be allied with the analytic rigor of concepts?

An earlier series of projects, published as *The Manhattan Transcripts* (Academy Editions—St. Martin's Press, 1981) was aimed at achieving a displacement of conventional architectural categories through a theoretical argument. La Villette was the built extension of a comparable method; it was impelled by the desire to move "from pure mathematics to applied mathematics." In its case, the constraints of the built realization both expanded and restricted the research. It expanded it, insofar as the very real economic, political and technical constraints of the operation demanded an ever increasing sharpening of the theoretical argumentation: the project became better as difficulties increased. But it restricted it insofar as La Villette had to be *built*: the intention was never merely to publish books or mount exhibitions; the finality of each drawing was "building": except in the book entitled *La Case Vide*, there were no "theoretical drawings" for La Villette.

However, the Parc de la Villette project had a specific aim: to prove that it was possible to construct a complex architectural organization without resorting to traditional rules of composition, hierarchy, and order. The principle of superimposition of three autonomous systems of points, lines and surfaces was developed by rejecting the totalizing synthesis of objective constraints evident in the majority of large-scale projects. In fact, if historically architecture has always been defined as the "harmonious synthesis" of cost, structure, use and formal constraints ("venustas, firmitas, utilitas"), the Park became architecture against itself: a dis-integration.

Our aims were to displace the traditional opposition between program and architecture, and to extend questioning of other architectural conventions through operations of superimposition, permutation and substitution to achieve "a reversal of the classical oppositions and a general displacement of the system," as Jacques Derrida has written, in another context, in *Marges*. Above all, the project directed an attack against cause and effect relationships, whether between form and function, structure and economics or (of course) form and program, replacing these oppositions by new concepts of contiguity and superimposition. "Deconstructing" a given program meant showing that the program could challenge the very ideology it implied. And deconstructing architecture involved dismantling its conventions, using concepts derived both from architecture and from elsewhere—from cinema, literary criticism and other disciplines. For if the limits between different domains of thought have gradually vanished in the past twenty years, the same phenomenon applies to architecture, which now entertains relations with cinema, philosophy and psychoanalysis (to cite only a few examples) in an intertextuality subversive of modernist autonomy. But it is above all the historical split between architecture and its theory that is eroded by the principles of deconstruction.

It is not by chance that the different systems of the Park negate one another as they are superimposed on the site. Much of my earlier theoretical work had questioned the very idea of structure, paralleling contemporary research on literary texts. One of the goals at La Villette was to pursue this investigation of the concept of structure, as expressed in the respective forms of the point grid, the coordinate axes (covered galleries) and the "random curve" (cinematic promenade). Superimposing these autonomous and completely logical structures meant questioning their conceptual status as ordering machines: the superimposition of three coherent structures can never result in a supercoherent megastructure, but in something undecidable, something that is the opposite of a totality. This device had been explored from 1976 onwards in *The Manhattan Transcripts*, where the overlapping of abstract and figurative elements (based on "abstract" architectonic transformations as much as on "figurative" extracts from the selected site) coincided with a more general exploration of the ideas of program, scenario and sequence.

The independence of the three superposed structures thus avoided all attempts to homogenize the Park into a totality. It eliminated the presumption of a pre-established causality between program, architecture and signification. Moreover, the Park rejected context, encouraging intertextuality and the dispersion of meaning. It subverted context: La Villette is anticontextual. It has no relation to its surroundings. Its plan subverts the very notion of borders on which "context" depends.

N O N - S E N S E / N O - M E A N I N G

The Parc de la Villette project thus can be seen to encourage conflict over synthesis, fragmentation over unity, madness and play over careful management. It subverts a number of ideals that were sacrosanct to the Modern period and, in this manner, it can be allied to a specific vision of postmodernity. But the project takes issue with a particular premise of architecture, namely, its obsession with presence, with the idea of a meaning immanent in architectural structures and forms which directs its signifying capacity. The latest resurgence of this myth has been the recuperation, by architects, of meaning, symbol, coding and "double coding," in an eclectic movement reminiscent of the long tradition of "revivalisms" and "symbolisms" appearing throughout history. This architectural postmodernism contravenes the reading evident in other domains, where postmodernism involves an assault on meaning or, more precisely, a rejection of a well-defined signified that guarantees the authenticity of the work of art. To dismantle meaning, showing that it is never transparent, but socially produced, was a key objective in a new critical approach that questioned the humanist assumptions of style. Instead, architectural postmodernism opposed the style of the Modern Movement, offering as an alternative another, more palatable style. Its nostalgic pursuit of coherence, which ignores today's social, political and cultural dissociations, is frequently the avatar of a particularly conservative architectural milieu.

The La Villette project, in contrast, attempts to dislocate and de-regulate meaning, rejecting the "symbolic" repertory of architecture as a refuge of humanist thought. For today the term "park" (like "architecture," "science," or "literature") has lost its universal meaning; it no longer refers to a fixed absolute, nor to an ideal. Not the *hortus conclusus* and not the replica of Nature, La Villette is a term in constant production, in continuous change; its meaning is

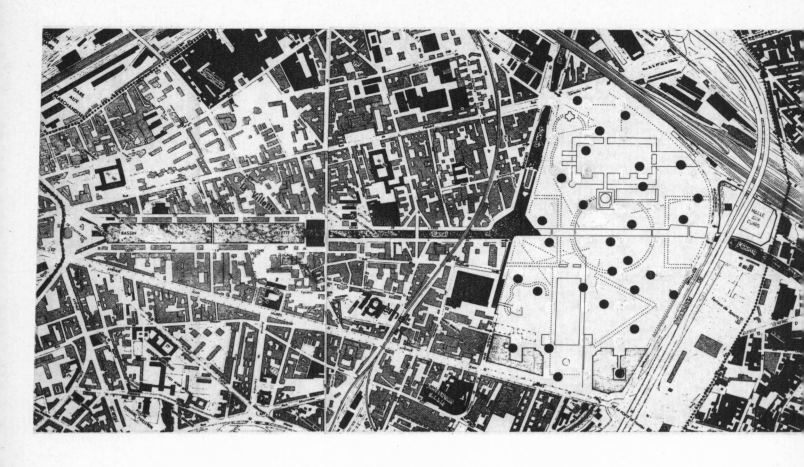

never fixed but is always deferred, differed, rendered irresolute by the multiplicity of meanings it inscribes. The project aims to unsettle both memory and context, opposing many contextualist and continualist ideals which imply that the architect's intervention necessarily refers to a typology, origin or determining signified. Indeed, the Park's architecture refuses to operate as the expression of a pre-existing content, whether subjective, formal or functional. Just as it does not answer to the demands of the self (the sovereign or "creative" architect) so it negates the immanent dialectic of the form, since the latter is displaced by superimpositions and transformations of elements that always exceed any given formal configuration. Presence is postponed and closure deferred as each permutation or combination of form shifts the image one step ahead. Most importantly, the Park calls into question the fundamental or primary signified of architecture—its tendency (as Derrida remarks in *La Case Vide*) to be "*in service*, and *at service*," obeying an economy of meaning premised on functional use. In contrast, La Villette promotes programmatic instability, functional *Folie*. Not a plenitude, but instead "empty" form: *les cases sont vides*.

La Villette, then, aims at an architecture that *means nothing*, an architecture of the signifier rather than the signified—one that is pure trace or play of language. In a Nietzschean manner, La Villette moves towards interpretive infinity, for the effect of refusing fixity is not insignificance, but semantic plurality. The Park's three autonomous and superimposed systems and the endless combinatory possibilities of the *Folies* give way to a multiplicity of impressions. Each observer will project his own interpretation, resulting in an account that will again be interpreted (according to psychanalytic, sociological or other methodologies) and so on. In consequence, there is no absolute "truth" to the architectural project, for whatever "meaning" it may have is a function of interpretation: it is not resident in the object, or in the object's materials. Hence, the "truth" of red *Folies* is not the "truth" of Constructivism, just as the "truth" of the system of points is not the "truth" of the system of lines. The addition of the systems' internal coherences is not coherent. The excess of rationality is not rational. La Villette looks out on new social and historical circumstances: a dispersed and differentiated reality that marks an end to the utopia of unity.

New York, Summer 1987

AN URBAN PARK FOR THE 21ST CENTURY

The competition for the Parc de La Villette is the first in recent architectural history to set forth a new program—that of the "Urban Park," proposing that the juxtaposition and combination of a variety of activities will encourage new attitudes and perspectives. This program represents an important breakthrough. The '70s witnessed a period of renewed interest in the formal constitution of the city, its typologies and its morphologies. While developing analyses focused on the history of the city, this attention was largely devoid of programmatic justification. No analysis addressed the issue of the activities that were to occur in the city. Nor did any properly address the fact that the organization of functions and events was as much an architectural concern as the elaboration of forms or styles.

The Parc de La Villette, in contrast, represents an open-air cultural center, encouraging an integrated programmatic policy related both to the city's needs and to its limitations. The program allocates space for workshops, gymnasium and bath facilities, playgrounds, exhibitions, concerts, scientific experiments, games and competitions, in addition to a Museum of Science and Technology and a City of Music. The Park could be conceived as one of the largest *buildings* ever constructed—a discontinuous building, but nevertheless a single structure, overlapping in certain areas with the city and existing suburbs. It forms an embryonic model of what the new programs for the 21st century will be.

During the 20th century we have witnessed a shift in the *concept* of the park, which can no longer be separated from the concept of the city. *The park forms part of the vision of the city.* The fact that Paris concentrates tertiary or professional employment argues against passive "esthetic" parks of repose in favor of new urban parks based on cultural invention, education and entertainment. The inadequacy of the civilization vs. nature polarity under modern city conditions has invalidated the time-honored prototype of the park as an image of nature. It can no longer be conceived as an undefiled Utopian world-in-miniature, protected from vile reality. What we see, then, is the exhaustion of the "open space" concept faced with the *reality* of the cultural park. Hence we oppose the notion of Olmsted, widespread throughout the 19th century, that "in the park, the city is not supposed to exist." To create false hills hiding the Périphérique ignores the power of urban reality.

1 ■ SITUATION PLAN 1982

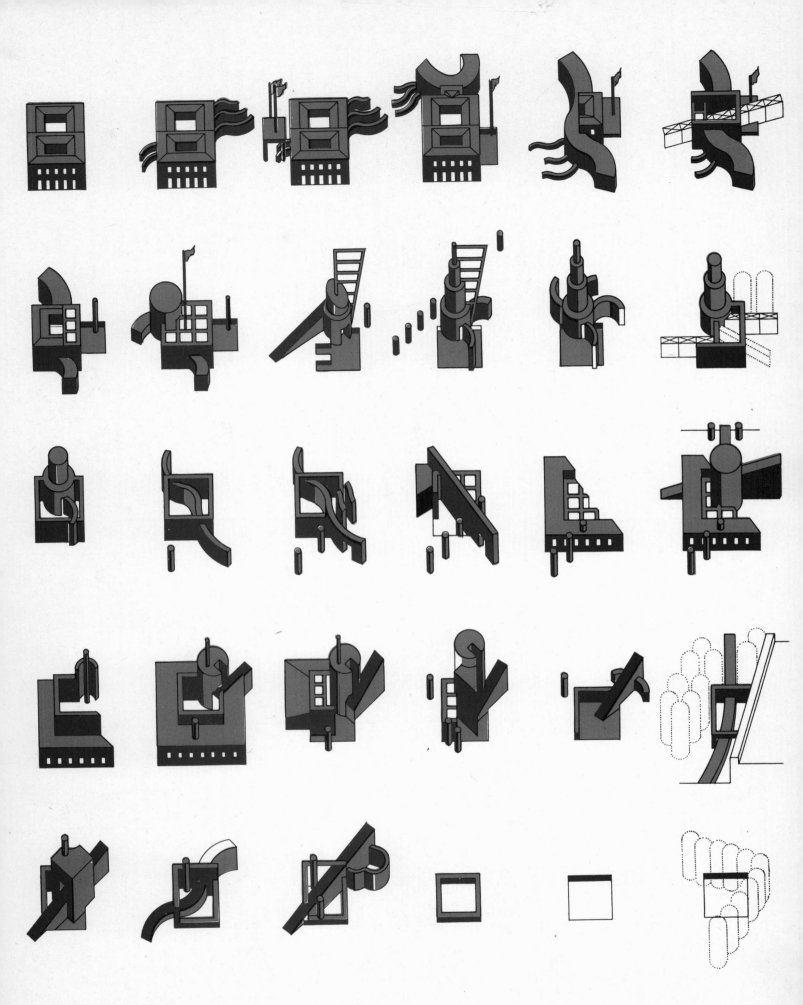

EARLY PRINCIPLE OF COMBINATION AND TRANSFORMATION OF ARCHITECTURAL ELEMENTS FROM THE POINT GRID OF FOLIES, DEVELOPED FROM AN EXISTING FIGURATIVE ELEMENT (AN 1865 PAVILLION ON THE SITE) TO AN ABSTRACT CUBE

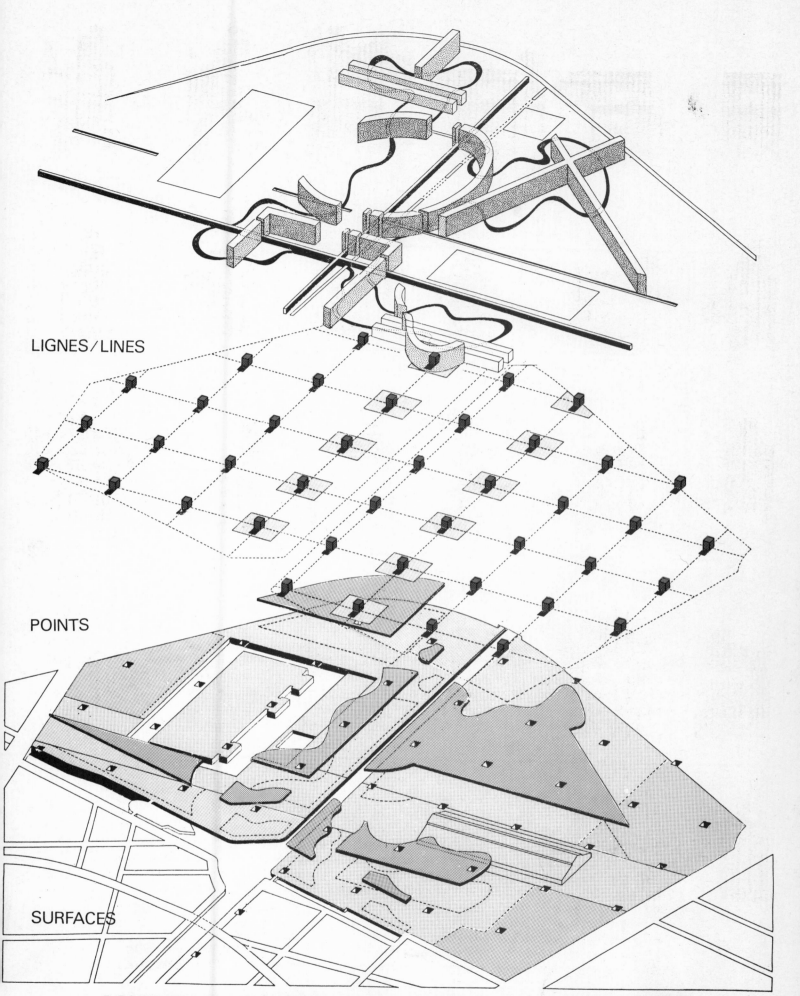

LIGNES / LINES

POINTS

SURFACES

THE SUPERIMPOSITION OF THE THREE SYSTEMS (POINTS, LINES, SURFACES) CREATES THE PARK AS IT GEN-
ERATES A SERIES OF CALCULATED TENSIONS WHICH REINFORCE THE DYNAMISM OF THE PLACE. EACH OF
THE THREE SYSTEMS DISPLAYS ITS OWN LOGIC AND INDEPENDENCE

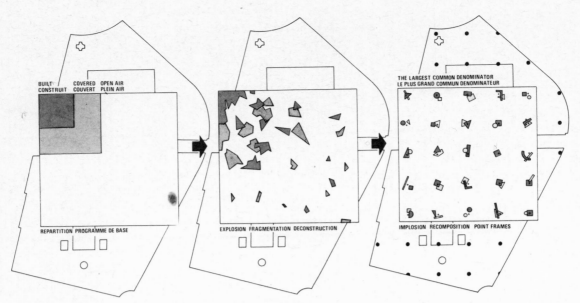

A SIMPLE STRUCTURAL SOLUTION: EXPLODING PROGRAMMATIC REQUIREMENTS THROUGHOUT THE SITE ONTO A REGULAR GRID OF POINTS OF INTENSITY (A MARK, A TRACE). HENCE THE DIFFERENT TYPES OF ACTIVITIES ARE FIRST ISOLATED AND THEN DISTRIBUTED ON THE SITE, OFTEN ENCOURAGING THE COMBINATION OF APPARENTLY INCOMPATIBLE ACTIVITIES (THE RUNNING TRACK PASSES THROUGH THE PIANO-BAR INSIDE THE TROPICAL GREENHOUSE)

A   N E W   M O D E L

We propose, instead, a distinctive and innovative kind of park, embodying a change in social context. Extending the radical shift in ideology implicit in the program, our ambition goes beyond producing a variation on an existing type by altering one of its components. We aim neither to change styles while retaining a traditional content, nor to fit the proposed program into a conventional mold, whether neo-classical, neo-romantic, or neo-modernist. Rather, our project is motivated by the most constructive principle within the legitimate "history" of architecture, by which new programmatic developments and inspirations result in new typologies. Our ambition is to create a new *model* in which program, form, and ideology all play integral roles.

S Y S T E M S   A N D   S U P E R I M P O S I T I O N S

Our project is motivated by the fact that the site is not "virgin land," but is located in a populated semi-industrial quarter, and includes two enormous existing structures, the Museum of Science and Technology and the Grand Halle. Rejecting the idea of introducing another mass, even of a linear character, into an already encumbered terrain and respecting the extensive requirements of the program, we propose a simple structural solution: to distribute the programmatic requirements over the total site in a regular arrangement of points of intensity, designated as *Folies*. Deconstructing the program into intense areas of activity placed according to existing site characteristics and use, this scheme permits maximum movement through the site, emphasizing discoveries and presenting visitors with a variety of programs and events.

Developments in architecture are generally related to cultural developments motivated by new functions, social relations or technological advances. We have taken this as axiomatic for our scheme, which aims to constitute itself as image, as structural model and as a paradigmatic example of architectural organization. Proper to a period that has seen the rise of mass production, serial repetition and disjunction, this concept for the Park consists of a series of related neutral objects whose very similarity allows them to be "qualified" by function. Thus in its basic structure each *Folie* is bare, undifferentiated and "industrial" in character; in the specialization of its program it is complex, articulated and weighted with meaning. Each *Folie* constitutes an autonomous sign that indicates its independent programmatic concerns and possibilities while suggesting, through a common structural core, the unity of the total system. This interplay of theme and variation allows the Park to read symbolically *and* structurally, while permitting maximum programmatic flexibility and invention.

In contrast to Renaissance or 19th century spatial organization, the Parc de La Villette presents a variation on a canonical modern spatial scheme, the *open plan*.

Conforming to the definition of a system or structure, the grid of the *Folies* is a self-referential,

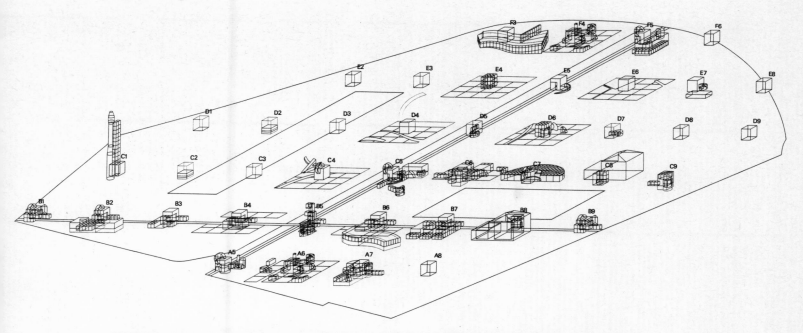

DISTRIBUTION OF BUILT MASSES THROUGHOUT THE SITE. THE FOLIES ARE BOTH SINGULAR POINTS AND ANCHORING POINTS OF POSSIBLE FUTURE CONSTRUCTIONS

meaning that it is initially independent of park, program and site. It is only when the grid is applied or, more precisely, *put in place*, that it takes on a reality distinguishing it from a simple geometric system.

The new park is formed by the encounter of three autonomous systems, each with its own logic, particularities and limits: the system of objects, the system of movements and the system of spaces. The overlay of the different systems thus creates a carefully staged series of tensions that enhances the dynamism of the park.

E T Y M O L O G Y

At its origin in seventeenth-century France, "*folie*" or folly had a meaning different from the one now assigned it at La Villette; it indicated an extravagant house of entertainment. In the 21st Century Urban Park, it loses such aristocratic connotations to gain a public image, while enlarging on contemporary psychoanalytic discoveries (in french, *la folie* means "madness," "insanity").

The new meaning of *folie* transforms its original sense by replacing the extravagant display of eclectic styles with the regulated juxtaposition of unprecedented programs. The purpose of this operation is to remove *la folie* from immersion in the historical object and to relocate it on the broader level of abstraction as an autonomous neutral object that subsequently receives the play of signs. Thus it is not the specific attributes of the object that are significant, but rather, its artificial abstraction—the closed perfection of the system to which the object refers. The *Folies* and their grid are fabricated forms, the products of processes by which abstraction (in this case, point, line, surface) has progressively come to replace reality. Substituting "culture" for "nature," they represent the gradual decline of the latter, and take their model from the repetitive capabilities and artificiality of the machine.

In this manner, the Urban Park can be seen to oppose the nineteenth-century concept of Nature, based on biological or physical laws, with the technologically-formed concept of the environment.

A Folie as homage to Borgès, Burroughs, Cocteau, Quenau and of course to Otto Julius Manntoifel, whose combinatory construction brought together "the revolving stage, the circulating library, the house as a living unit, the winter garden, some flawless allegorical marbles, the Roman Catholic chapel, the Buddhist temple, the skating rink, frescoes, the polyphonic organ, the currency exchange, the men's room, the Turkish bath, and the wedding cake—to mention only a few of its elements. The burdensome maintenance of this multiple structure, however, caused it to be auctioned off and dismantled almost immediately following the festivities which crowned its opening." (J.L. Borgès, A. Bioy Casarès, Chronicles of Bustos Domecq).

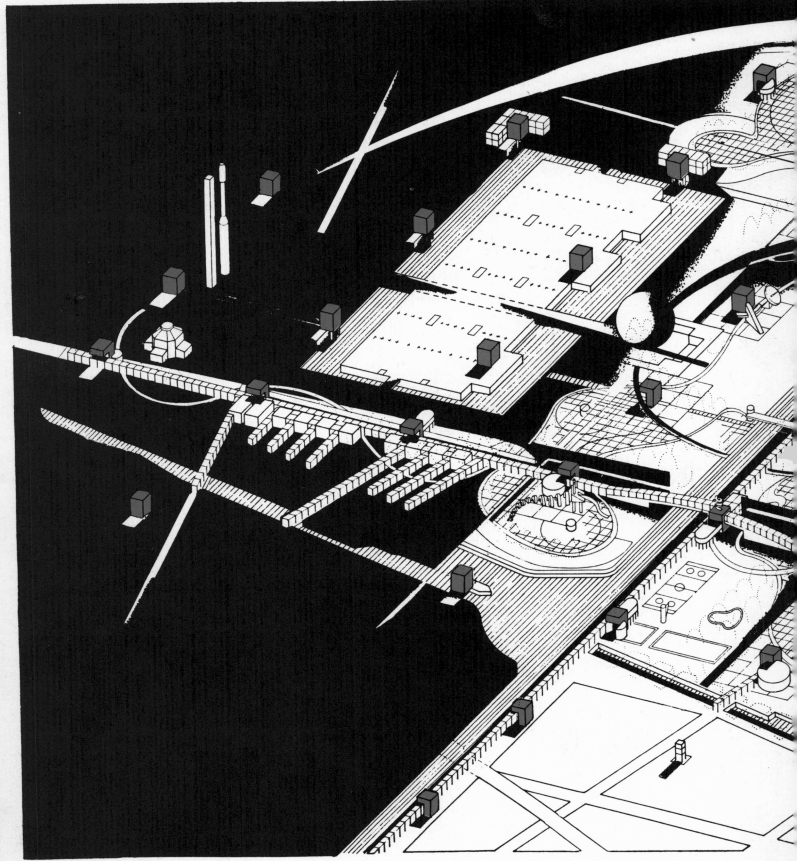

POINTS
THE PROGRAMMATIC NEEDS FIRST HAVE BEEN EXPLODED INTO A SERIES OF FRAGMENTS. THESE FRAG-
MENTS ARE THEN DISTRIBUTED AROUND A SINGLE BUILT COMMON DENOMINATOR: THE POINT GRID OF
FOLIES

LINES
THE PEDESTRIAN MOVEMENTS ARE QUALIFIED BY 1) TWO COORDINATE AXES, OR COVERED PERPENDICU-
LAR GALLERIES, 2) A MEANDERING "CINEMATIC" PROMENADE THAT RELATES VARIOUS PARTS OF.THE
PARK IN A SEQUENTIAL MANNER, 3) ALLEYS OF TREES LINKING THE KEY ACTIVITIES ON THE SITE

SURFACES
THE VARIOUS PARK SURFACES HAVE THEIR OWN TEXTURES, CORRESPONDING TO THEIR RESPECTIVE PRO-
GRAMMATIC NEEDS (PAVEMENTS, GRASS, SPORTS)

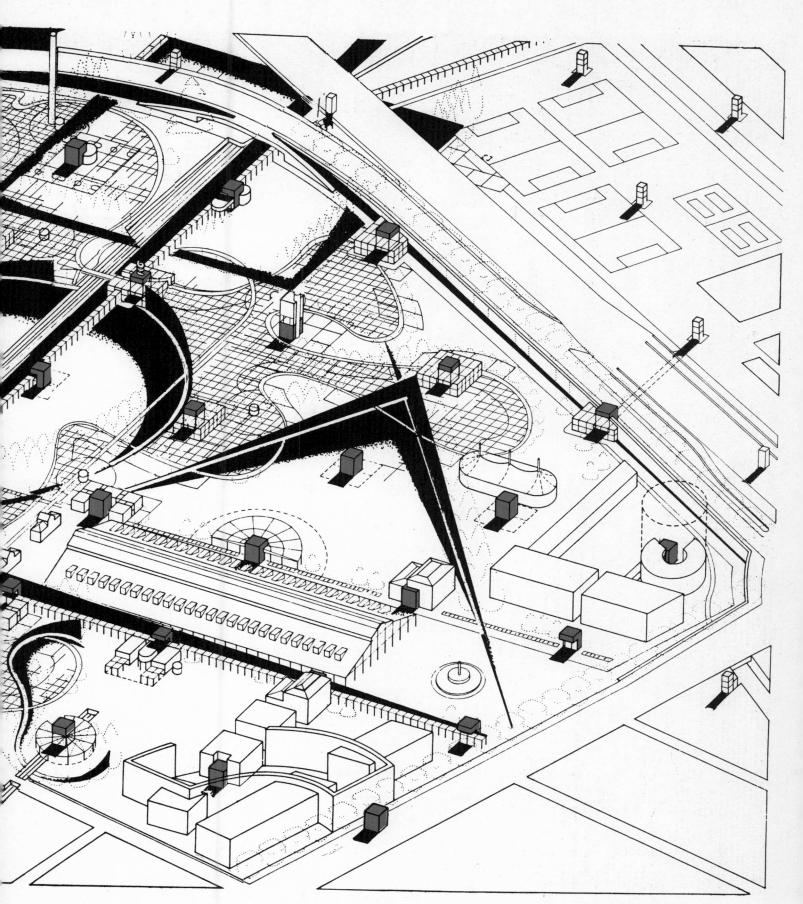

P O I N T S   L I N E S   S U R F A C E S

Points   point-like activities
Lines   linear activities
Surfaces   surface activities

POINTS

The *Folies* are placed according to a point-grid coordinate system at 120-meter intervals. They provide a common denominator for all events generated by the program. Each is essential for the program. Each is essentially a 10 x 10 x 10 meter cube or a three-story construction of neutral space which can be transformed and elaborated according to specific programmatic needs.

The strict repetition of the basic 10 x 10 x 10 meter *Folie* is aimed at developing a clear *symbol* for the Park, a recognizable identity as strong as the British telephone booth or the Paris Metro gates.

The advantages of this grid system are manifold. It is by far the simplest system establishing territorial recognition and one that is easily implemented. It lends itself to easy maintenance.

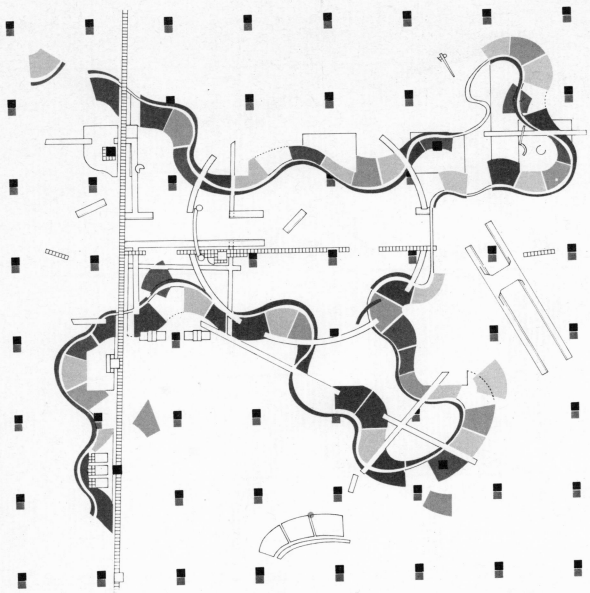

THE CINEMATIC PROMENADE OF GARDENS: A MONTAGE OF SEQUENCES AND FRAMES CONCEIVED AS SPACES FOR THE INTERVENTIONS OF ARTISTS, LANDSCAPE DESIGNERS, ARCHITECTS AND PHILOSOPHERS. THE PROMENADE OF GARDENS IS DESIGNED AS A FILM STRIP, IN WHICH THE SOUNDTRACK CORRESPONDS TO THE PEDESTRIAN PATH AND THE IMAGE TRACK TO THE SUCCESSIVE FRAMES OF SPECIFIC GARDENS AIMED AT SUCH ACTIVITIES AS BATHING, PICNICKING, ROLLERSKATING, AS WELL AS FOR DISPLAYING THE STAGING OF "NATURAL" PLANTING OR CONCEPTUAL GARDENS (GARDENS BY DESIGNERS)

The structure provides a comprehensive image or shape for an otherwise ill-defined terrain. The regularity of routes and positioning makes orientation simple for those unfamiliar with the area. The advantage of the point grid system is that it provides for the *minimum adequate equipment* of the urban park relative to the number of its visitors.

LINES
The *Folie* grid is related to a larger coordinate structure (the Coordinates) an orthogonal system of high-density pedestrian movement which marks the site with a cross. The North-South Passage or Coordinate links the two Paris gates and subway stations of Porte de la Villette and Porte de Pantin; the East-West Coordinate joins Paris to its suburbs. A 5 meter wide, open covered structure runs the length of both Coordinates. Organized around the Coordinates so as to facilitate and encourage access are *Folies* designated for the most frequented activities: the City of Music, restaurants, Square of the Baths, art and science displays, children's playgrounds, video workshops and Sports Center.
The Line system also includes the *Path of Thematic Gardens*, the seemingly random curvi-linear route that links various parts of the Park in the form of a carefully planned circuit. The Path of Thematic Gardens intersects the Coordinate axes at various places, providing unexpected encounters with unusual aspects of domesticated or "programmed" nature.

SURFACES
The *surfaces* of the Park receive all activities requiring large expanses of horizontal space for play, games, body exercises, mass entertainment, markets, etc. Each surface is programmatically determined. So-called left-over surfaces (when every aspect of the program has been fulfilled) are composed of compacted earth and gravel, a park material familiar to all Parisians. Earth and gravel surfaces allow for complete programmatic freedom.

Excerpts from the architect's report to the International Jury, 1983.

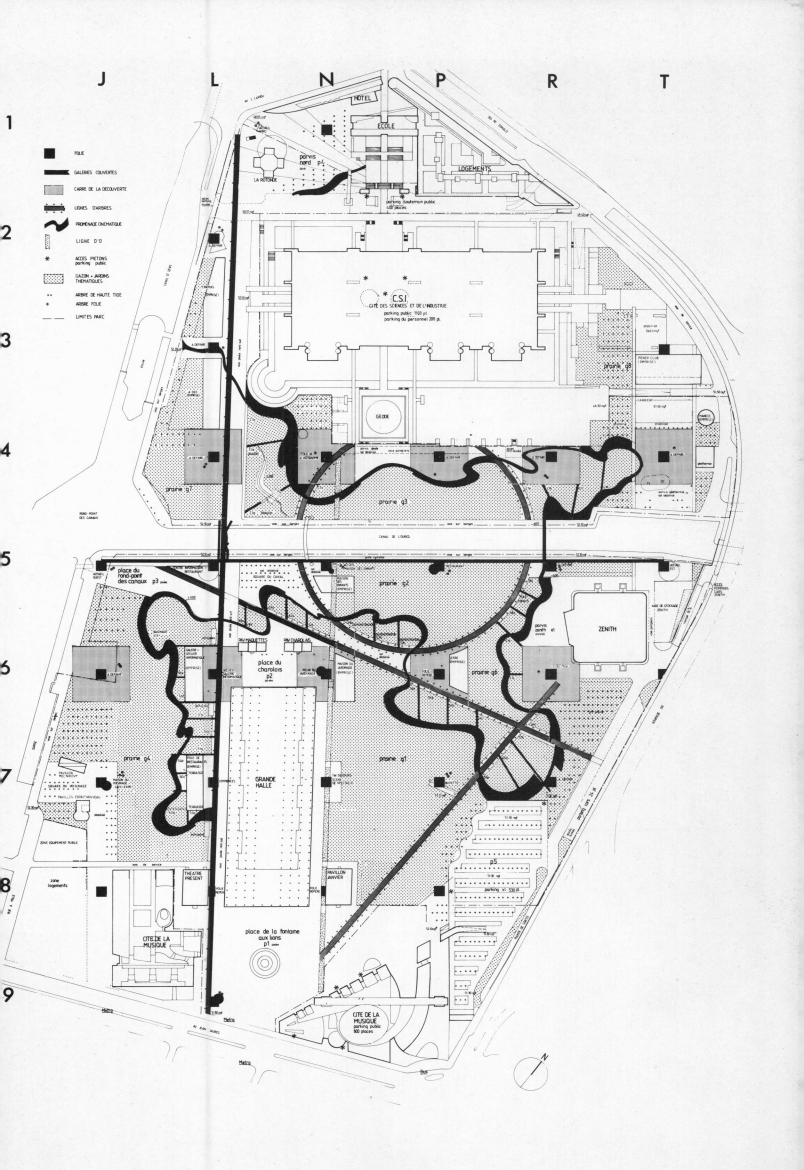

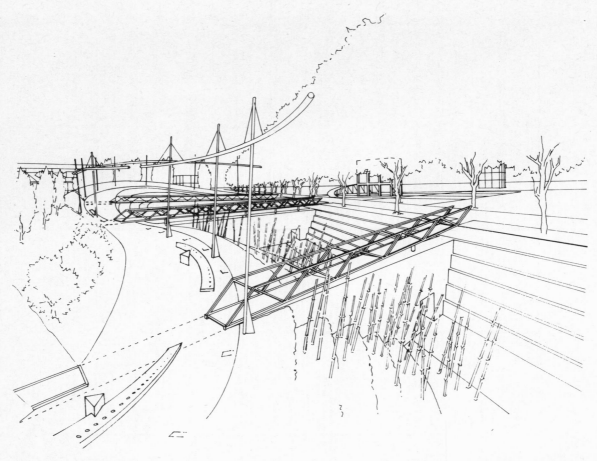

CINEMATIC PROMENADE WITH 1) ALUMINUM CATWALKS THAT DELINEATE THE FRAMES OF SUCCESSIVE SEQUENCES, 2) A BLUISH-GREEN NEON CURVILINEAR STRIP SUSPENDED FROM ALUMINUM MASTS AND 3) FLUORESCENT SPOTS ON LONG GREY-BLUE ARTIFICIAL "STONE" BENCHES

F R A M E S   A N D   S E Q U E N C E S

The Cinematic Promenade is one of the key features of the Park. It is conceived along the analogy of a film strip in which the sound-track corresponds to the general walkway for visitors and the image-track corresponds to the successive frames of individual gardens. *The linearity of sequences orders events, movements and spaces in a progression that either combines or parallels divergent concerns. Each part, each frame of a sequence qualifies, reinforces or alters the parts that precede and follow it. The associations thus formed allow for a plurality of interpretations rather than a singular fact. Each part is thus both complete and incomplete.* If the general structure of the sequence of gardens requires the indetermination of its content (hence the role of the chief architect as film director overseeing the montage of sequences), its specific content implies determinacy (through the particular designs of individual designers). *The Park is also inhabited: sequences of events, use, activities, incidents are inevitably super-imposed on those fixed spatial sequences. It suggests secret maps and impossible fictions, rambling collections of events all strung along a collection of spaces, frame after frame, garden after garden, episode after episode.*

At La Villette a frame means each of the segments of the sequence: in the cinematic promenade, each frame defines a garden. Each of these frames can be turned into a single piece of work.

The framing principle permits arrangement of each part of the sequence since, as with the cinegrams of a film, each frame can be infinitely mixed, combined, superimposed, etc. More-over, the content of each frame can be shown from above or from below, producing unusual viewpoints. The spatial sequences at La Villette can also be seen independently from the meanings they may suggest. Their signification can be deduced directly from the events occur-ring in the sequence (a row of slides, a sand box and a rollerskating space undoubtedly imply a children's sequence).

In literature and in the cinema the relations between frames or between sequences can be manipulated through devices such as flashbacks, jumpcuts, dissolves and so on. Why not in architecture or in landscape? At La Villette, the cut between two garden sequences is exe-cuted by means of a line of trees. In other words, the lines of trees defining the "triangle" and the "circle" are to be read first as cuts between sequences. *All sequences are cumulative. Their "frames" derive significance from juxtaposition. They establish memory—of the preced-ing frames.*

Excerpt from "Etude de Définition," unpublished, Paris 1984.

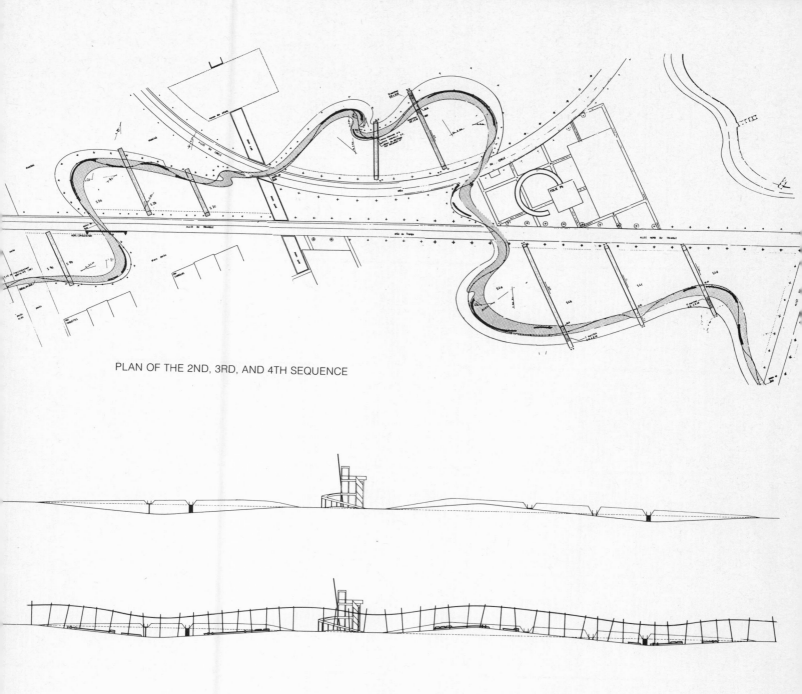

PLAN OF THE 2ND, 3RD, AND 4TH SEQUENCE

RHYTHMS: SIMULTANEITY OF FRAMES, LIGHTING STRIP AND PROMENADE PLANTING

"RHYTHMS"
USE MOVEMENTS

"MELODIES"
SPATIAL AMBIANCES

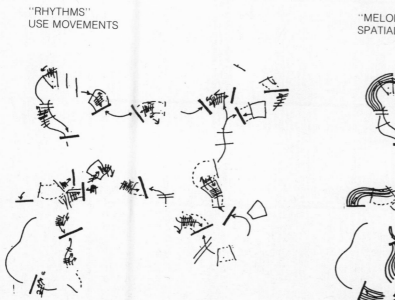

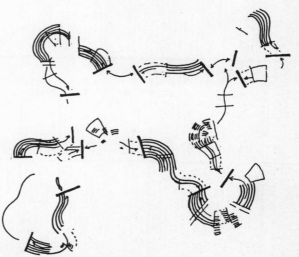

SUPERIMPOSITION (LANDSCAPE: POINTS, LINES, SURFACES) 1984

CINEMATIC PROMENADE. THE 4TH SEQUENCE 1984

LINE OF 0, CINEMATIC PROMENADE AND FOLIE OF SPECTACLES 1984

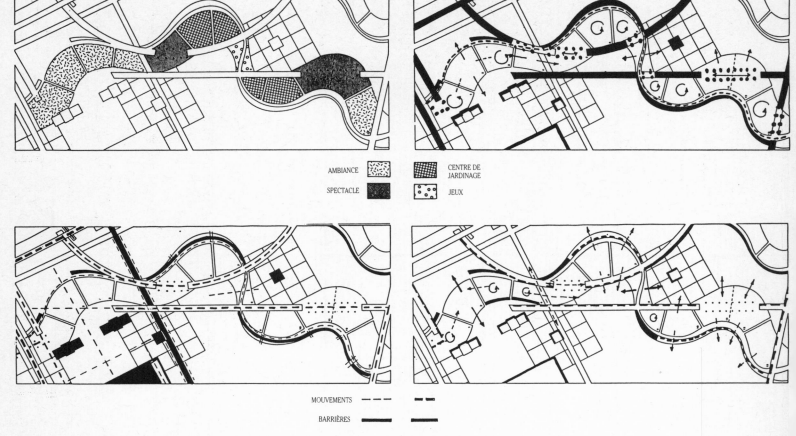

AMBIANCE
SPECTACLE
CENTRE DE JARDINAGE
JEUX

MOUVEMENTS
BARRIÈRES

PRINCIPES DE MONTAGE DES DIFFÉRENTS CADRAGES DE LA PROMENADE CINÉMATIQUE

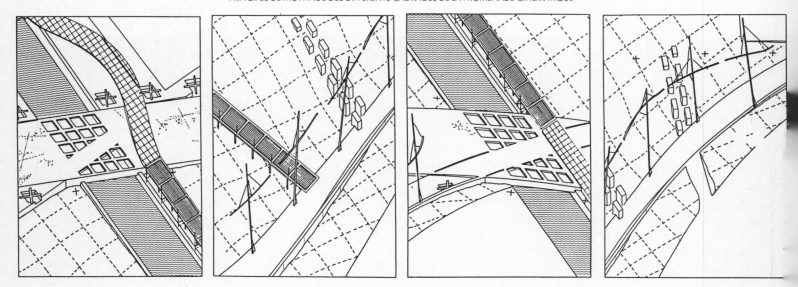

DETAILS OF THE SUPERIMPOSITION OF THREE DIFFERENT SYSTEMS (POINTS, LINES, SURFACES). EXTRACTS SHOWING THE INTERSECTION OF THE CINEMATIC PROMENADE WITH THE ALLEYS OF TREES AND THE LINE OF 0

C O N C E P T   O F   F O L I E
(M A D N E S S   A N D   T H E   C O M B I N A T I V E)

MADNESS

"Madness would then be a word in perpetual discordance with itself and interrogative throughout, so that it would question its own possibility, and therefore the possibility of the language that would contain it; thus it would question itself, since the latter also belongs to the game of language." (Maurice Blanchot)

Madness serves as a constant point of reference throughout the Urban Park of La Villette because it appears to illustrate a characteristic situation at the end of the twentieth century—that of disjunctions and dissociation between use, form and social values. This situation is not necessarily a negative one, but rather is symptomatic of a new condition, as distant from eighteenth century humanism as from this century's various modernisms. Madness, here, is linked to its psychoanalytical meaning—insanity—and can be related to its built sense—folly—only with extreme caution. We aim to free the built *Folie* from its historical connotations and to place it on a broader, more abstract plane, as an autonomous object which, in the future, will be able to receive new meanings.

It is not necessary to recall in this context how Michel Foucault, in *Madness and Civilization*, analyzes the manner in which insanity raises questions of a sociological, philosophical, and psychoanalytic nature. If I suggest that madness also raises an architectural question, it is in

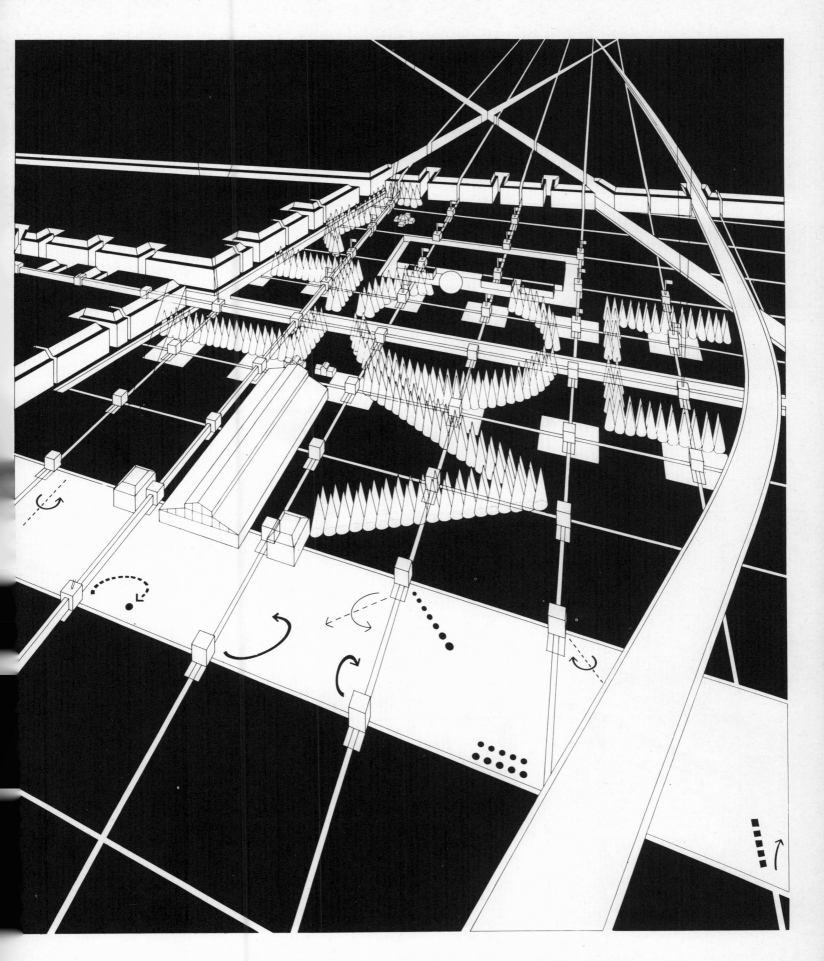

order to demonstrate two points. On the one hand, that normality ("good" architecture: typologies, Modern Movement dogmas, Rationalism, and other "isms" of recent history) is only one possibility among those offered by the combination, the "genetics" of architectural elements. On the other, that, just as all societies require lunatics, deviants, and criminals to mark their own negativity, so architecture needs extremes and interdictions to inscribe the reality of its constant oscillation between the pragmatics of the built realm and the absoluteness of concepts. There is no intention here to descend into an intellectual fascination with madness, but rather to stress that madness articulates something that is often negated in order to preserve a fragile cultural or social order.

In this analogy, the contemporary city and its many parts (here La Villette) are made to correspond with the dissociated elements of schizophrenia. The question becomes that of knowing one's relationship to such dislocated city parts. Our hypothesis, here, is that this relationship necessarily suggests the idea of transference. Transference in architecture resembles the psychoanalytic situation, the tool through which theoretical reconstruction of the totality of

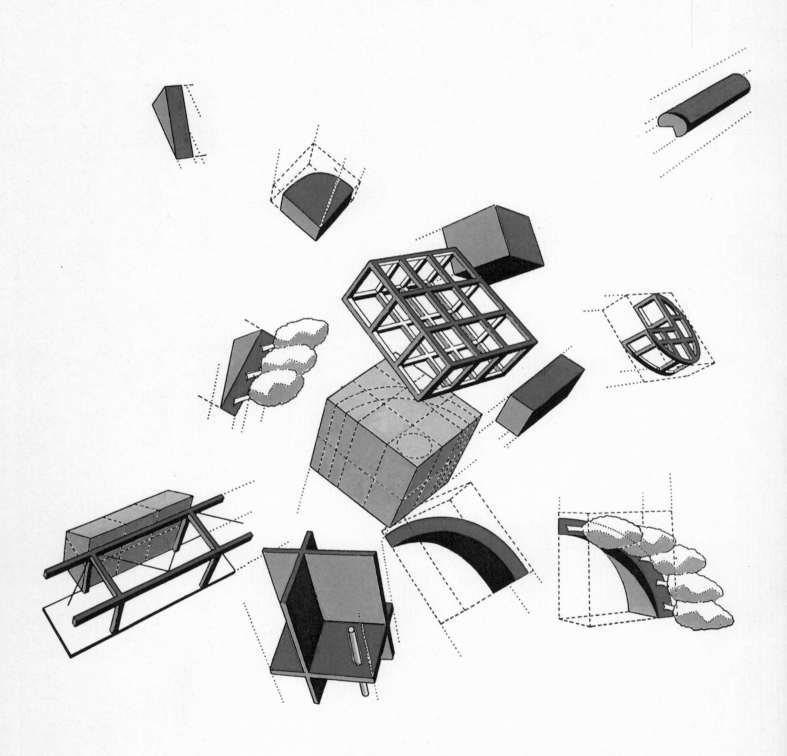

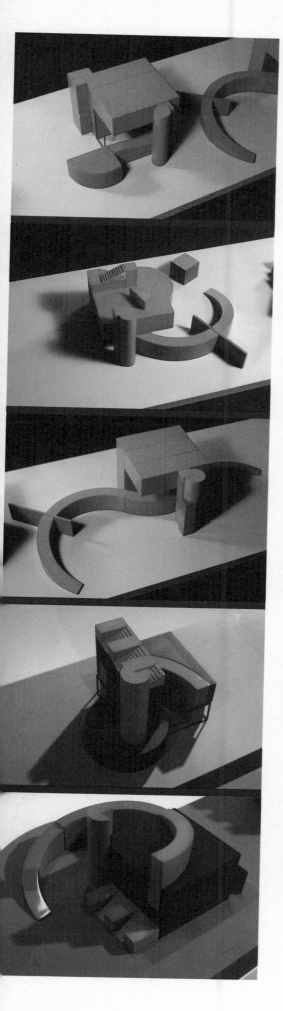

FOLIE L5

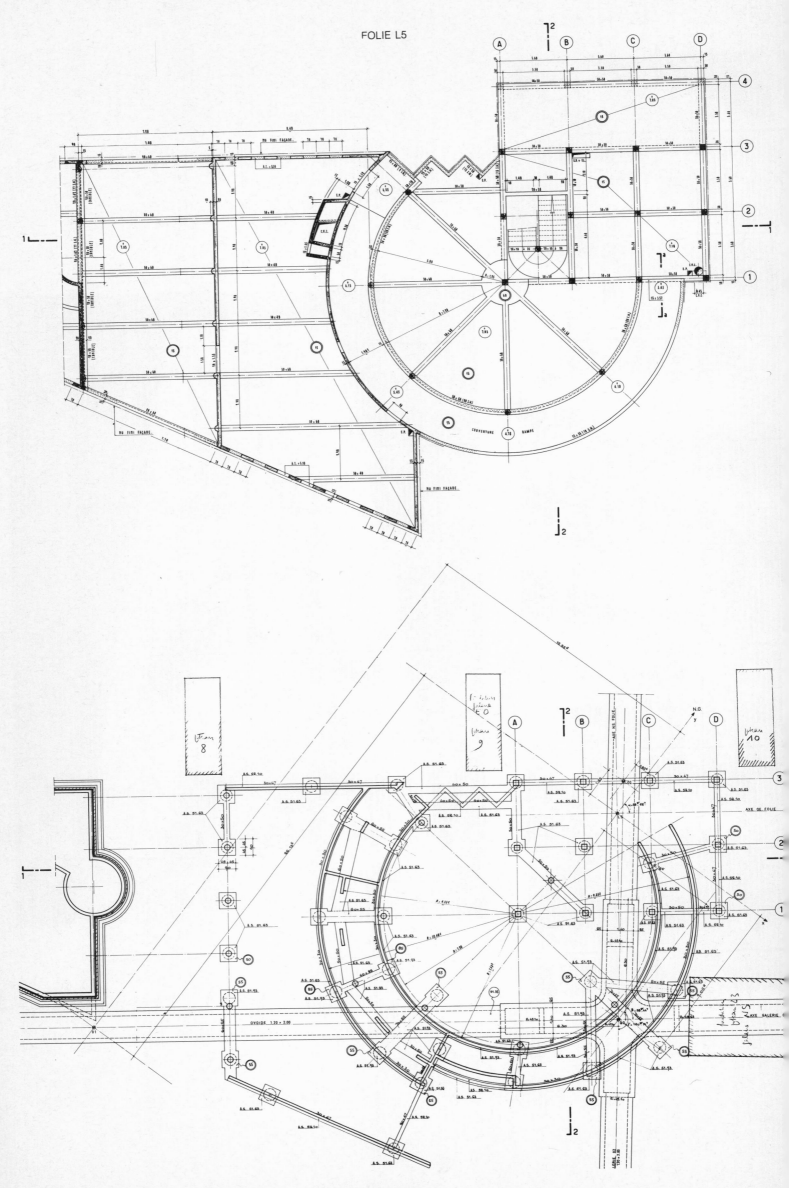

STRUCTURAL SYSTEM AND FOUNDATIONS 1985 ■ 20

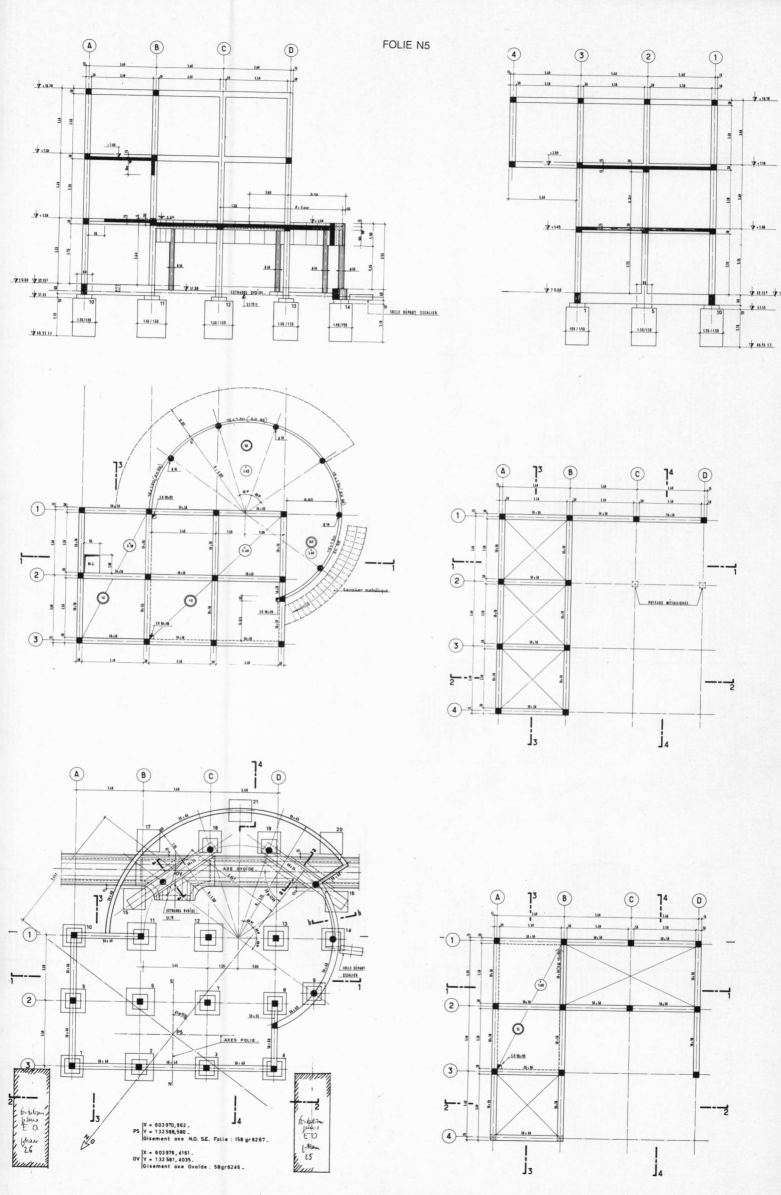

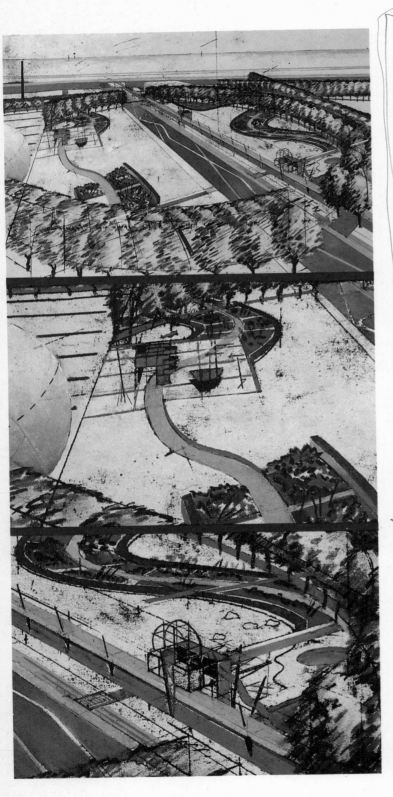
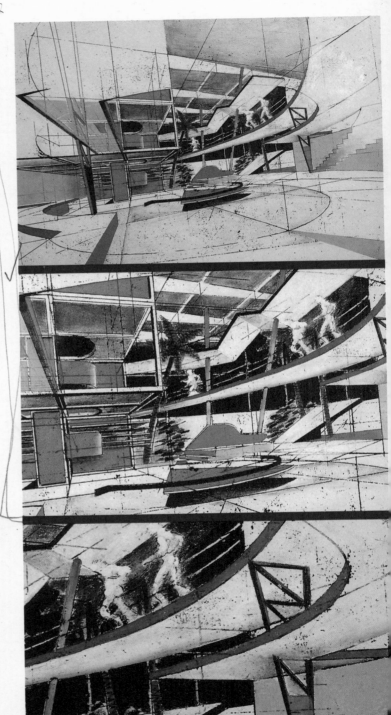

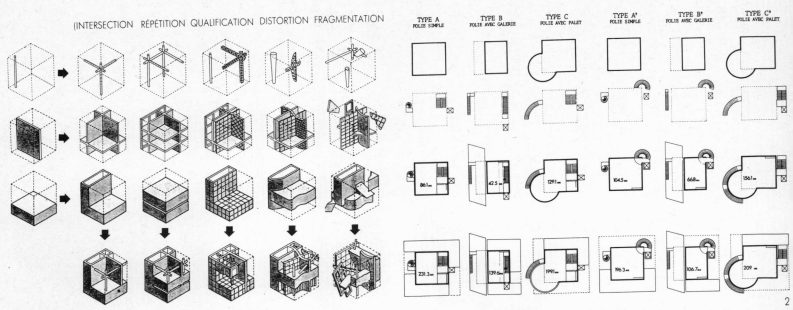

TYPE A FOLIE SIMPLE   TYPE B FOLIE AVEC GALERIE   TYPE C FOLIE AVEC PALET   TYPE A' FOLIE SIMPLE   TYPE B' FOLIE AVEC GALERIE   TYPE C' FOLIE AVEC PALET

1. WALLS AND INTERIOR PLANES (SOLID WALLS, CURTAIN WALLS, TRELLIS) CAN BE COMBINED ACCORDING TO SPECIFIC RULES (INTERSECTION, REPETITION, QUALIFICATION, DISTORTION, FRAGMENTATION)

2. A TYPOLOGY OF POSSIBLE SURFACES AND CONFIGURATIONS AT THE USERS DISPOSAL

OPPOSITE PAGE: COMBINATION OF FOLIES BASED ON THE PRINCIPLE OF THE *CASE VIDE* (THE VOID IN EACH MATRIX): EACH FOLIE IS THE RESULT OF THE INTERSECTON BETWEEN SPACES, MOVEMENTS AND EVENTS. VERTICALLY: ORGANIZATION OF SPACE AND MOVEMENT CONFIGURATIONS—TYPE A: SIMPLE FOLIE. TYPE B: FOLIE WITH GALLERY. TYPE C: EXTENDED FOLIE. HORIZONTALLY: FROM THE TOP—FIRST LINE: INTRODUCING "INDUSTRIAL" COMPONENTS; SECOND LINE: "URBAN" COMPONENTS; THIRD LINE: "NATURE" COMPONENTS

the subject is attempted. "Transference is taken here as transport: dissociation explodes transference into fragments of transference." In the La Villette project, we speak of a "formalization," an acting-out of dissociation. In a psychoanalytical situation, the transference fragments are transported to the psychotherapist. In an architectural situation, these transference fragments can only be transported onto architecture itself. The approach behind La Villette suggests meeting points, anchoring points where fragments of dislocated reality can be apprehended.

In this situation, the formation of the dissociation requires that a support be structured as a point of reassembly. The point of the *Folie* becomes the focus of this dissociated space; it acts as a common denominator, constituting itself as a system of relations between objects, events, and people. It allows the development of a charge, a point of intensity.

The grid of *Folies* permits the combination of places of transference on the background of the La Villette site. Obviously, it is secondary to try to determine in advance the architectural forms that are most appropriate to such transferential situations. All that counts is that the *Folie* is both the place and the object of transference. This fragmentary transference in madness is nothing but the production of an ephemeral regrouping of exploded or dissociated structures.

The point grid is the strategic tool of the La Villette project. It both articulates space and activates it. While refusing all hierarchies and "compositions," it plays a political role, rejecting the ideological *a priori* of the masterplans of the past. The Urban Park at La Villette offers the possibility of a restructuring of a dissociated world through intermediary space—*Folies*—in which the grafts of transference can take hold.

The point grid of *Folies* constitutes the place of a new investment. The *Folies* are new markings: the grafts of transference. These transference grafts allow access to space: one begins with an ambivalence toward a form in space which must be "reincarnated." The *Folies* create a "nodal point where symbol and reality permit the building of the imaginary by reintroducing a dialectic of space and time." The park at La Villette offers such a transition space, a form of access to new cultural and social forms in which expression is possible, even when speech has disappeared.

La Villette, then, can be seen as an innovative exposition of a technique on the level of superpositions and anchoring points. It offers places to apprehend objects and uses. It "builds itself into a mechanism that acts as reassembling unit for all the modes of locating." It is a surface of multireferential anchoring points for things or people which leads to a partial coherence, yet challenges the institutional structure of official culture, urban parks, museums, leisure centers, etc.

COMBINATION

"Although every creation is of necessity combinative, society, by virtue of the romantic myth of 'inspiration' cannot stand being told so." Roland Barthes, *Sade, Fourier, Loyola*.

The fragmentation of our contemporary, "mad" condition inevitably suggests new and unforeseen regroupings of its fragments. No longer linked in a coherent whole, independent from their past, these autonomous fragments can be recombined through a series of permutations whose rules have nothing to do with those of classicism or modernism.

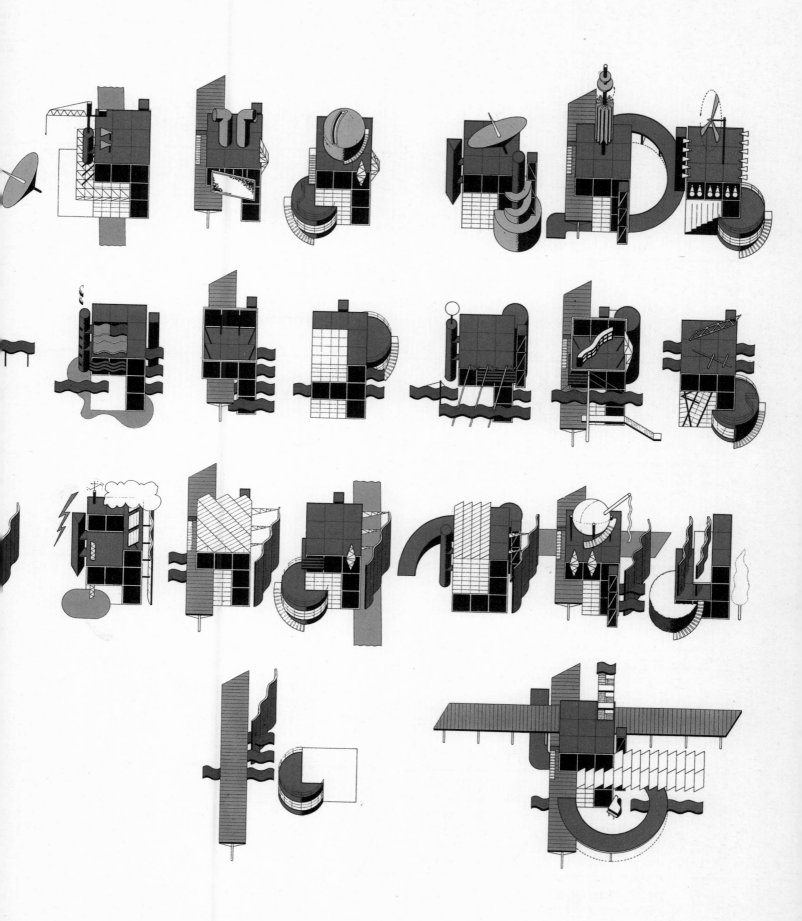

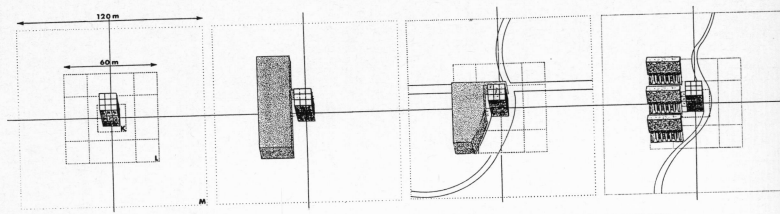

URBANISTIC CONCEPT: AS THE POINT GRID OF FOLIES IS DESIGNED AND BUILT BY BERNARD TSCHUMI, CHIEF ARCHITECT OF THE PARK, OTHER DESIGNERS MAY BUILD ADJACENT CONSTRUCTIONS

The argument behind our La Villette project attempts to demonstrate, first, that any "new" architecture implies the ideas of combination, that all form is the result of combination. It then proceeds to indicate that the notion of combination can be articulated into different categories. It should be emphasized that architecture is not seen here as the result of composition, a synthesis of formal concerns and functional constraints, but rather as part of a complex process of transformational relations.

Our purpose is not to propose the kind of new moral or philosophical role often associated with architectural endeavors. Instead, we aim to consider the architect first as a formulator, an inventor of relations. We also aim to analyze what will be called in this context the "combinative," that is, the set of combinations and permutations that is possible among different categories of analysis (space, movement, event, technique, symbol, etc.), as opposed to the more traditional play between function or use and form or style.

In this perspective, architecture is regarded as no longer concerned with composition or the expression of function. Instead, it is seen as the object of permutation, the combination of a large set of variables, which is meant to relate, either in a manifest or secret way, domains as different as the act of running, double expansion joints, and the free plan. Such a play of permutations is not gratuitous. It permits new and hitherto unimagined activities to occur. However, it also implies that any attempt to find a new model or form of architecture requires an analysis of the full range of possibilities, as in the permutational matrices used by research scientists and structuralists alike. Indeed, perhaps the most important legacy of structuralism has to do with heuristics, demonstrating that meaning is always a function of both position and surface, produced by the movement of an empty slot in the series of a structure.

The guiding principle of reseach on La Villette is precisely that of the empty slot. This play of permutations was initially explored in *The Manhattan Transcripts;* "the football player skates on the battlefield" was the manifesto of the interchangeability of objects, people, and events. Influenced by poststructuralist texts as much as by the different techniques of film montage, the *Transcripts* were only introducing, in a theoretical manner, what is to be applied at La Villette.

In a remarkable study entitled *Palimpsestes*, the literary critic Gérard Genette has refined these concepts of transformation. Combination, he writes, exists only within a complex system of transformational relations. These relations can act on whole texts as much as on fragments. In the case that concerns us, that of La Villette, a general type of transformation called *"mechanical operations"* can be distinguished. Mechanical operations may take several forms: a) that of "lexical" permutations, as in the decomposition of the 10m x 10m x 10m cube of the original *Folie* into a series of discrete fragments or elements, i.e., square or rectangular rooms, ramps, cylindrical stairs, etc., which have been ordered to form a catalogue or lexicon. A lexical permutation entails taking an element from the original cube and mechanically replacing it with another from the lexicon (for example, e + 7: each element of the cube is exchanged for the element of the lexicon placed in seventh position behind it); or b) that of "hypertextual" permutation, by which an element of the cube will be replaced by another—for example, by a nineteenth-century Neo-Classical pavilion placed nearby on the site. Such transplantation may lead to a semantic transformation in terms of its new context.

A series of transformations and permutations similar to the f2"oulipian" manipulations of the writers Queneau and Perec derives from the notion of the mechanical operation. This mixing technique, generally known as "contamination," can take innumerable forms. It is characterized by the purely mechanical aspect of the transformation, thus distinguishing it from pastiche or parody, which carefully divert a text from its initial context toward a use with a meaning known well in advance. No semantic intention governs the transformation of La Villette; they result from the application of a device or formula. While this may superficially resemble a variation on the Surrealist *"exquisite corpse,"* we have seen earlier that the relation between form and meaning is never one between signifier and signified. Architectural relations are never semantic, syntactic or formal, in the sense of formal logic. Instead, a better analogy to these montage and mixing techniques might be found in Vertov's or Eisenstein's work in the cinema, Queneau's in literature, or in the infinite variations around an initial theme that one finds in J.S. Bach's *Fugues*.

However, were this process only to involve deriving transformations and permutations on the level of the solid elements of architecture, such as walls, stairs, windows, and moldings, it would not differ significantly from most research on modes of composition or transformation as

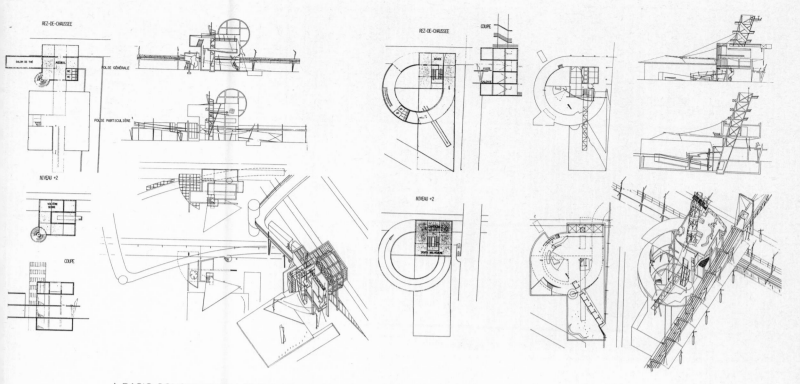

A BASIC CONSTRUCTION (THE CUBE) BEGINNING WITH A "NORMAL" CONFIGURATION AND THEN DEVIATING FROM IT ACCORDING TO COMBINATION DEVICES INDICATED EARLIER

Programmatic combination of folies:
L5:   cinéma-restaurant,   piano-bar,   vidéo theater,   observatory, shops,   running track,   possibly small   radio studio.   N5: children's folie,   drawing workshop,   tarzan-bar,   slide,   water games,   the administration.   N7:   folie of spectacles,   water wheel,   first aid clinic.

such. In contrast, and in opposition to functionalist, formalist, classical, and modernist doctrines, our ambition, already expressed in *The Manhatten Transcripts*, is to deconstruct architectural norms in order to reconstruct architecture along different axes; to indicate that space, movement and event are inevitably part of a minimal definition of architecture, and that the contemporary disjunction between use, form and social values suggests an interchangeable relation between object, movement and action. In this manner, the program becomes an integral part of architecture and each element of this program becomes an element of permutation akin to solid elements.

Excerpts from "Madness and Combinative," Bernard Tschumi in *Precis*, Columbia Architecture Journal, New York, Fall 1984.

S T R U C T U R A L   S Y S T E M   O F   T H E   F O L I E S

All of the *Folies* use the same repetitive system, based on 10.8 meter by 10.8 meter by 10.8 meter (36 x 36 x 36 foot) cube. The cube is then divided in three in each direction, forming a cage with 3.6 meters (12 feet) between bars.

The cage can be decomposed into fragments of a cage or extended through the addition of other elements (one- or two-story cylindrical or triangular volumes, stairs, ramps) according to a variety of combinatory principles, while simultaneously (and independently) confronting specific programmatic requirements. The primary structure (the cage) is composed of a frame which can be concrete or steel—or any other material, for that matter. The selection of the structural material is made according to fire code requirements or economic conditions. A red enamelled steel envelope covers every part of the structural frame. It is designed so as to solve every interior or exterior corner, cantilever or edge condition.

Although the *Folies* proceed from a simple construction principle, deviation alters the relationship to the structural grid. The grid then becomes a simple support around which a transgressive architecture can develop in relation to the original norm. The relationship between normality and deviation suggested a method for the elaboration of the *Folies*: First, requirements and constraints derived from the program are confronted with the architectonic combination and transformation principles of the project. The confrontation results in a basic architectural state: the "norm." Then, the norm is transgressed—without, however, disappearing. A distortion of the original norm results: deviation.

Deviation is both the excess of rationality and irrationality. As a norm, it contains the components of its own explosion. As a deviation, it frees them. Normality tends towards unity, deviation towards heterogeneity and dissociation. This is not a coupling of opposites but, instead, a matter of degree. How are these degrees of deviation determined? Through economy, time, money, circumstances, client's demands. A "normal" *Folie* is not built in the same manner as a "deviant" one.

FOLIE N5

FOLIE P7

FOLIE N7

29 ■ FOLIES P6, P5. MODELS 1985

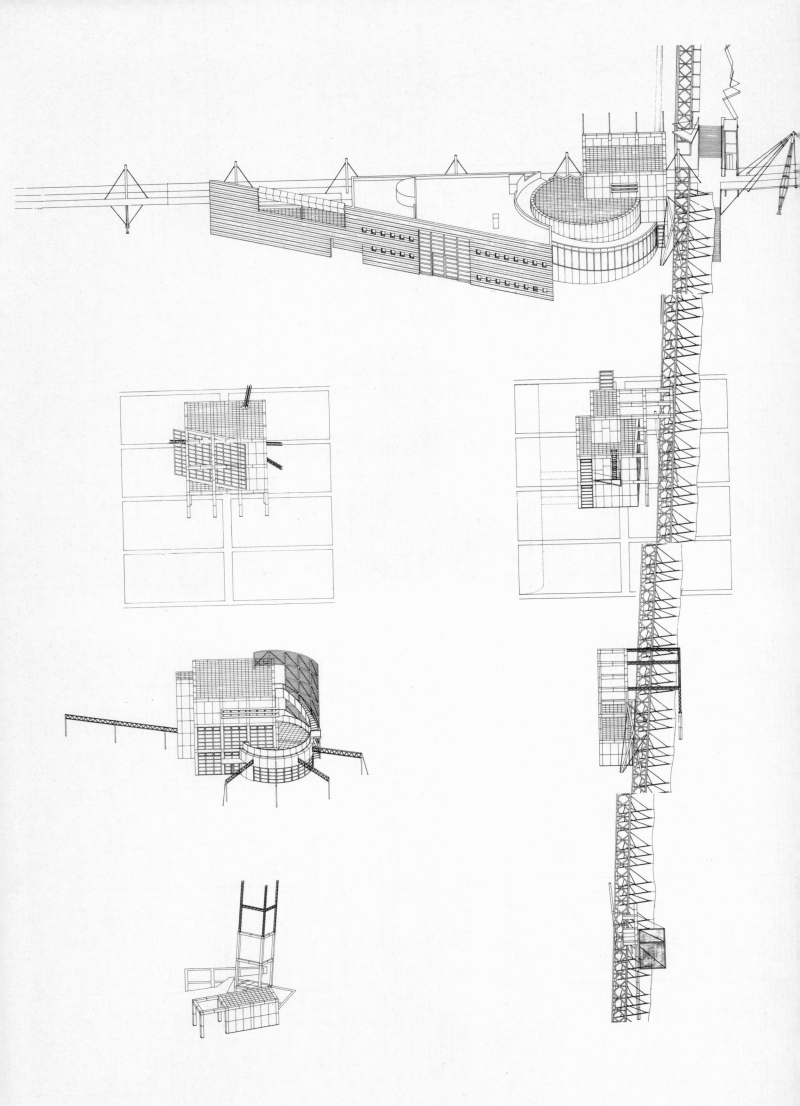

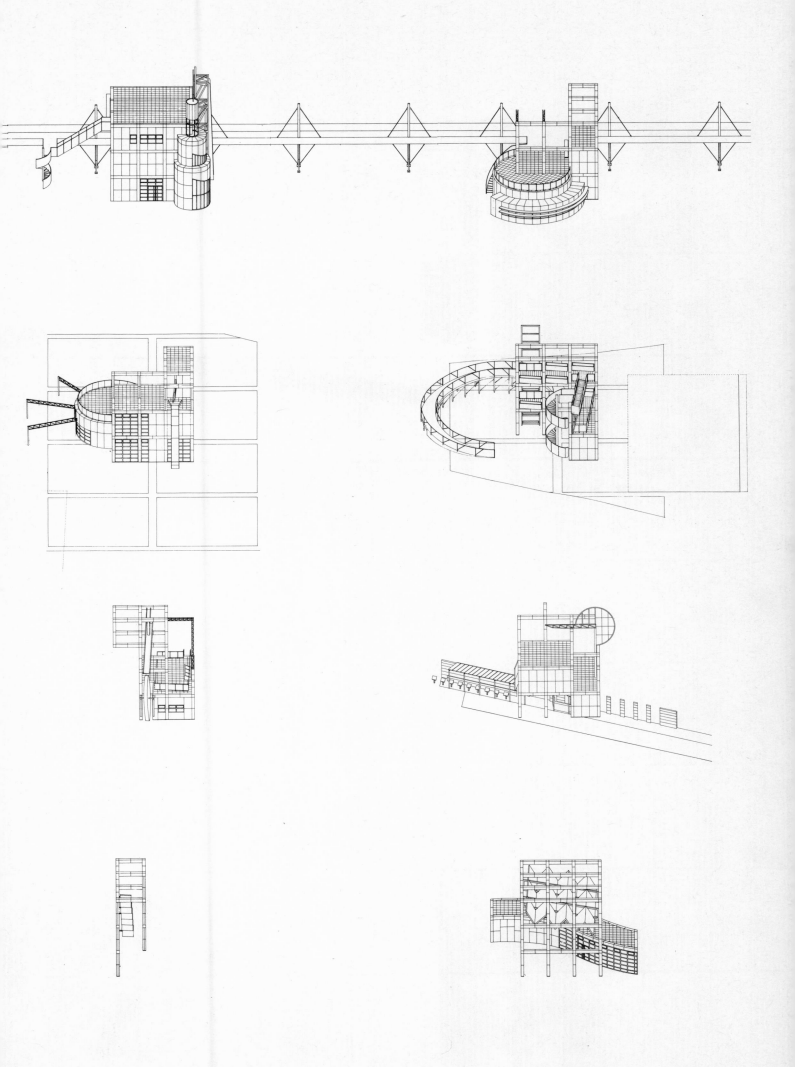

FOLIE N5

FOLIE J7

FOLIE P6

FOLIE L3. PLANS LEVEL +2. LEVEL 0. SECTION

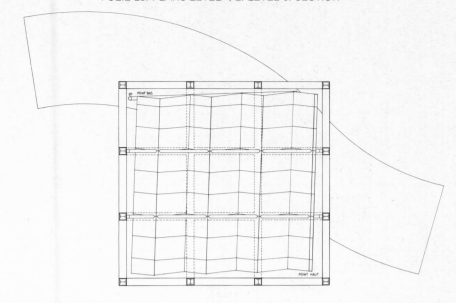

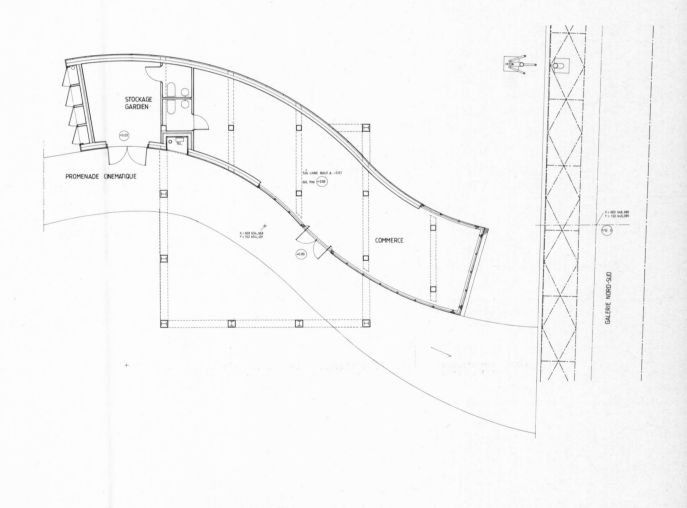

STOCKAGE
GARDIEN

PROMENADE CINEMATIQUE

COMMERCE

GALERIE NORD-SUD

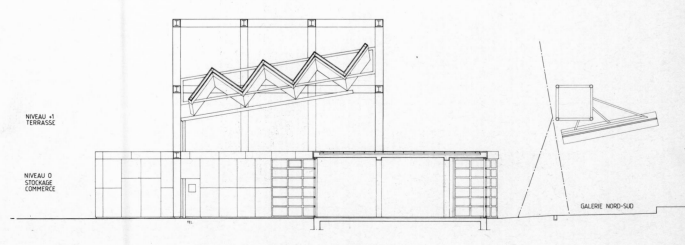

NIVEAU +1
TERRASSE

NIVEAU 0
STOCKAGE
COMMERCE

GALERIE NORD-SUD

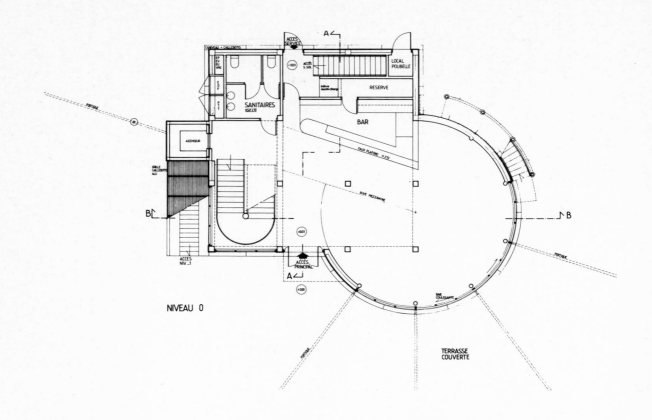

NIVEAU 0

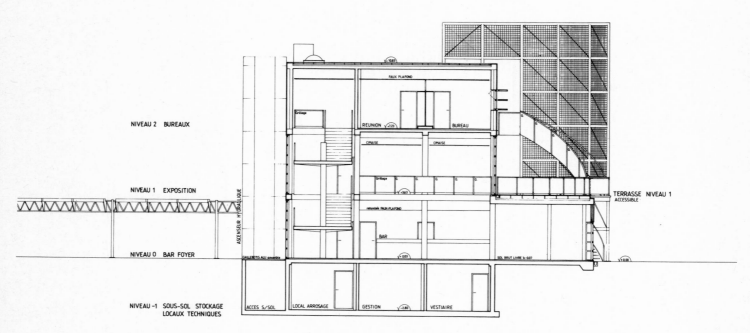

NIVEAU 2 BUREAUX

NIVEAU 1 EXPOSITION

NIVEAU 0 BAR FOYER

NIVEAU -1 SOUS-SOL STOCKAGE
LOCAUX TECHNIQUES

TERRASSE NIVEAU 1
ACCESSIBLE

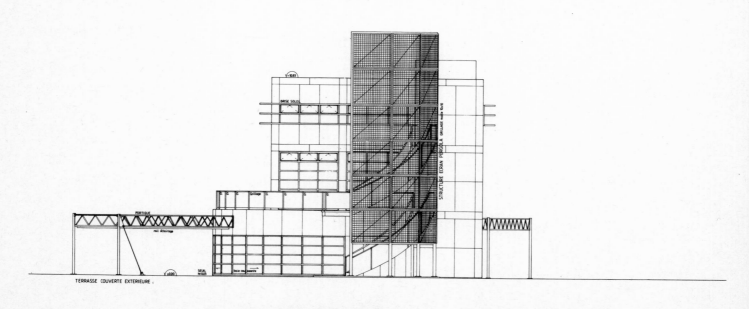

FOLIE R6. PLAN LEVEL +2. SECTION. NORTH ELEVATION

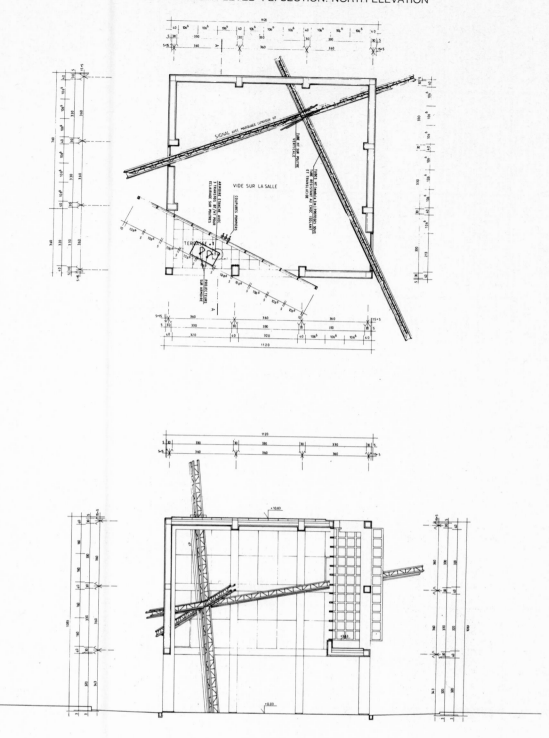

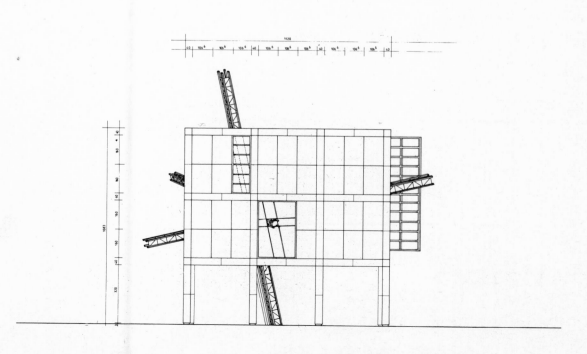

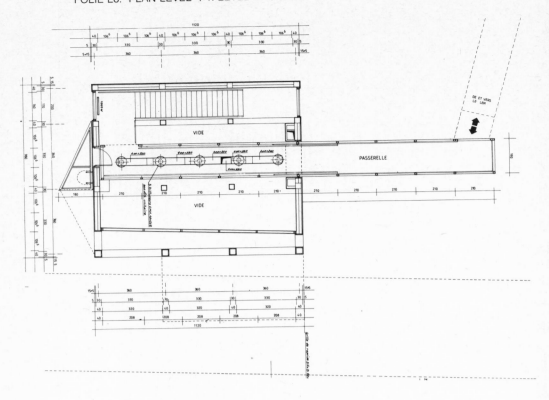

VIDE

VIDE

PASSERELLE

DE ET VERS
LE LEM

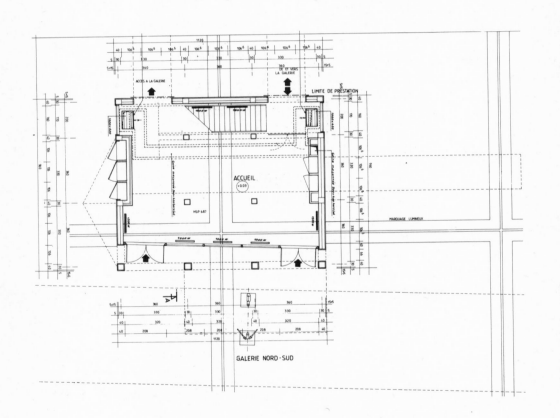

ACCÈS A LA GALERIE

DE ET VERS
LA GALERIE

LIMITE DE PRESTATION

ACCUEIL
+0.03

HSP 687

MARQUAGE LUMINEUX

GALERIE NORD·SUD

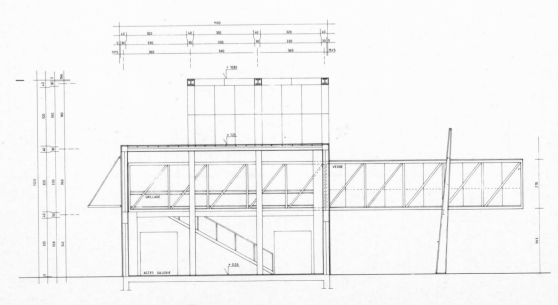

GRILLAGE

VERRE

ACCÈS GALERIE

+0.03

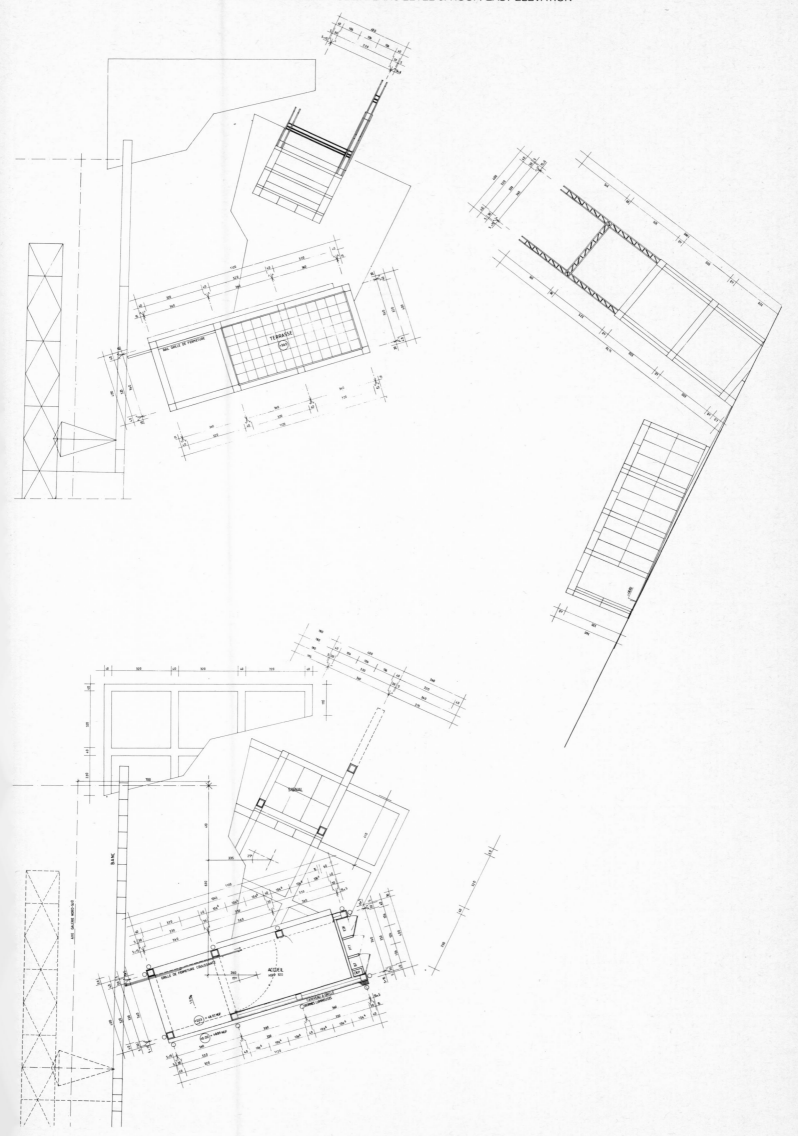

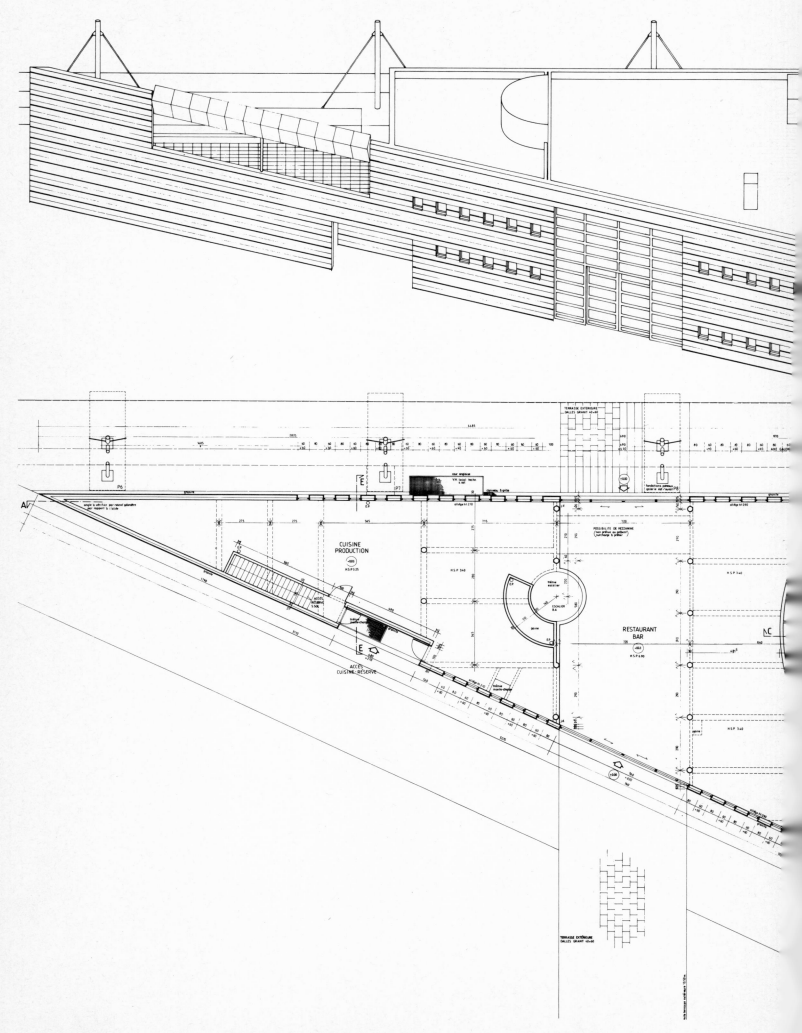

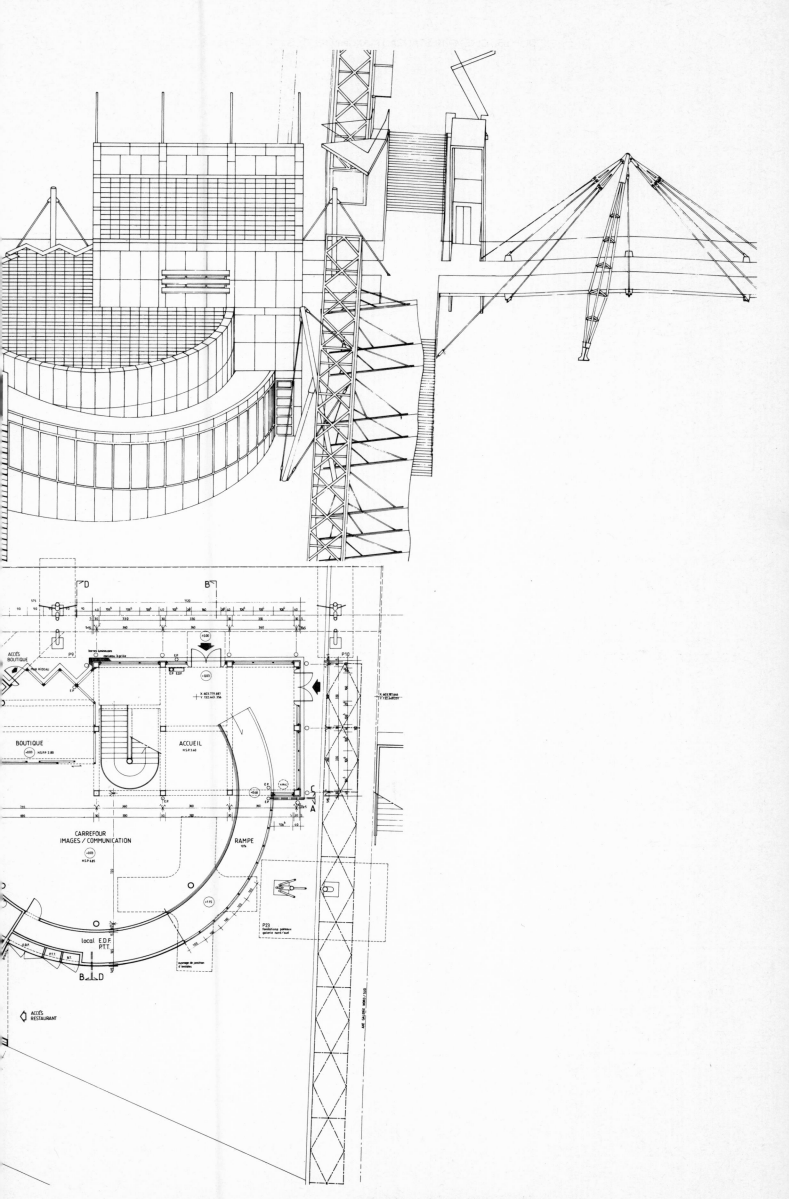

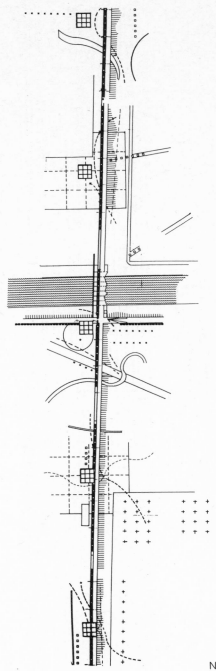

NORTH-SOUTH GALLERY. NOTATION

STRUCTURAL SYSTEM OF THE GALLERIES

If the system of points of intensity throughout the Park materializes through the grid of *Folies*, the system of lines is characterized by the Cinematic Promenade, the alleys of trees and, in particular, by the covered North-South and East-West galleries which act as coordinate axes of the site. Nearly one kilometer long, linking the Porte de Pantin to the Porte de la Villette, the North-South Gallery is a brilliantly-lit public street, open 24 hours a day and connecting the urban functions of the park: the Museum of Science and Industry, Cinema-*Folies*, Restaurant-*Folies*, Video-*Folies*, the 19th century Grande Hall, a theater, the City of Music. The breaks in scale that can be observed on such a trajectory suggested that one could take advantage of occasional changes in ground level by keeping the main supporting beam of the Gallery rigorously horizontal, hence increasing its standard height of 5.4 meters (18 feet) to 9 meters (30 feet) near the gigantic Museum of Science and Industry. The length of the Gallery (of which perhaps no comparable example exists anywhere in the world), as well as the concept of a "floating" superimposed element, suggested long 21.6 meter (65-foot) spans between vertical supports which contrast architecturally and historically with the 8 meter (24-foot) span of the 19th-century Grand Hall. Consistent with the principle of autonomy of the Park's various conceptual systems, the construction module of the main beam differs from the grid of the undulating canopy it supports. This principle of superimposition finds its most spectacular expression in the carefully orchestrated collisions between the North-South Gallery and the *Folies* it meets on its trajectory. Parallel to the distorted parallelogram of the Grand Halle rather than to the orthogonal grid of *Folies*, the Gallery collides four times with *Folies*, thus determinig their respective architecture.

The East-West Gallery along the Canal de l'Ourcq not only extends the monumental route that leads from Ledoux's Rotonda to the suburbs but also acts as an elevated track, a sort of balcony overlooking the Park and the Museum of Science and Industry and giving second-floor access to the *Folies* located along the Canal. Again, the interpenetration of the East-West Gallery and the *Folies* it encounters qualifies the cantilevered architecture of these *Folies*.

41 ■ AXONOMETRIC VIEW. NORTH-SOUTH GALLERY 1985

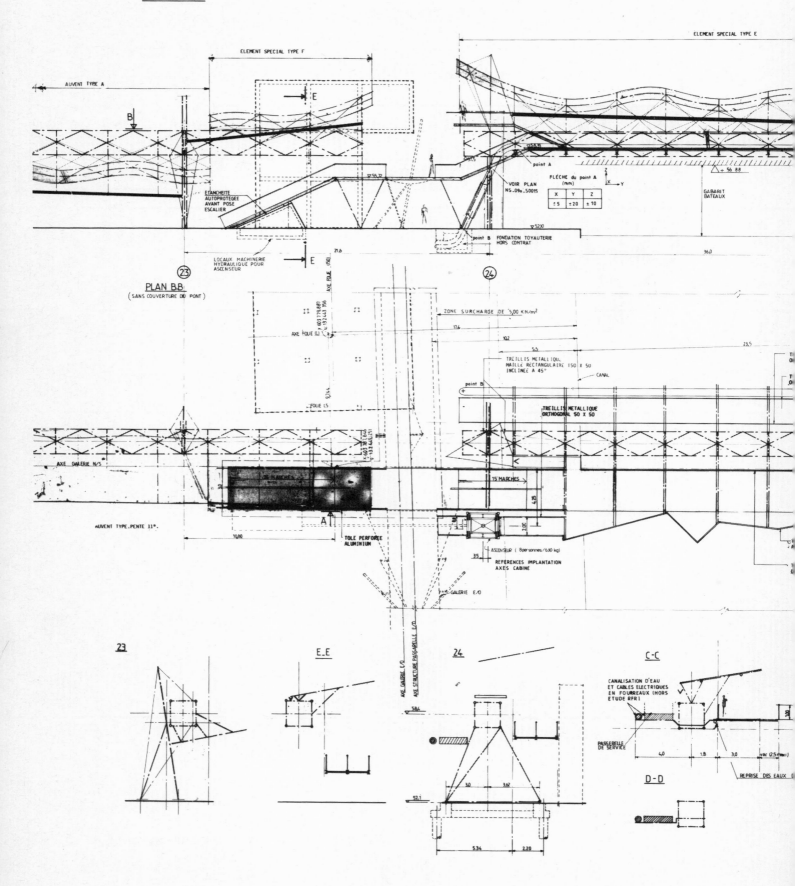

ELEVATION A-A

PLAN B.B
(SANS COUVERTURE DU PONT)

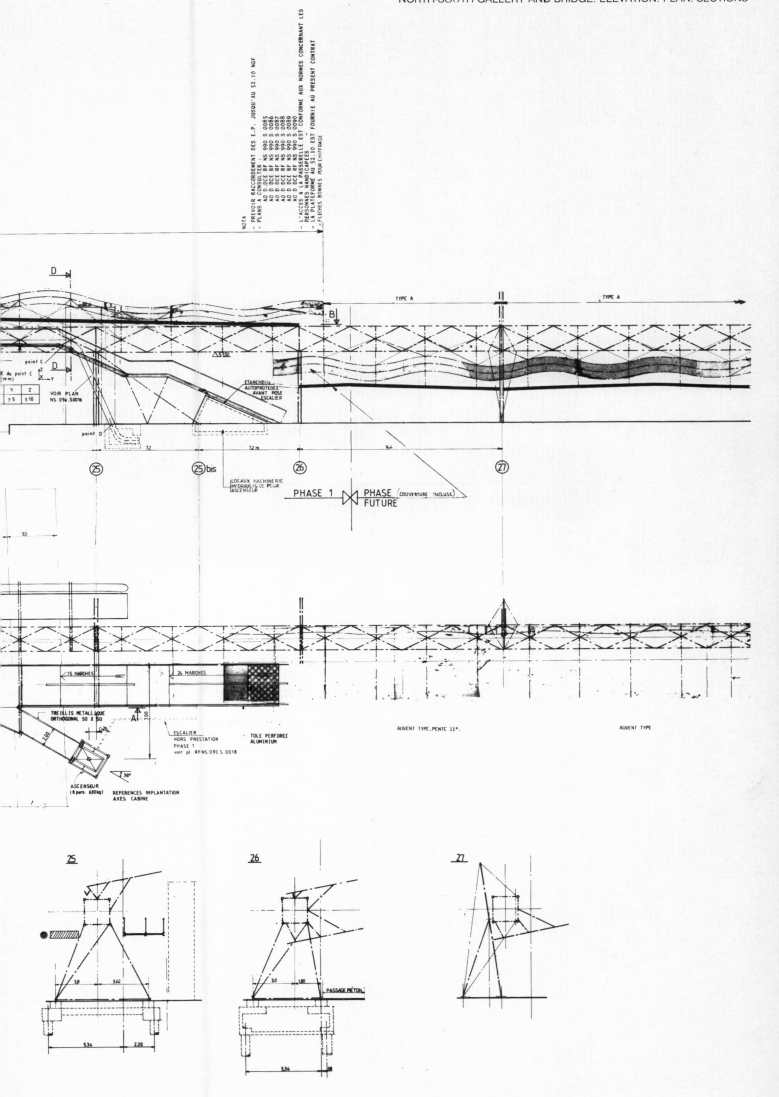

NORTH - SOUTH GALLERY AND BRIDGE

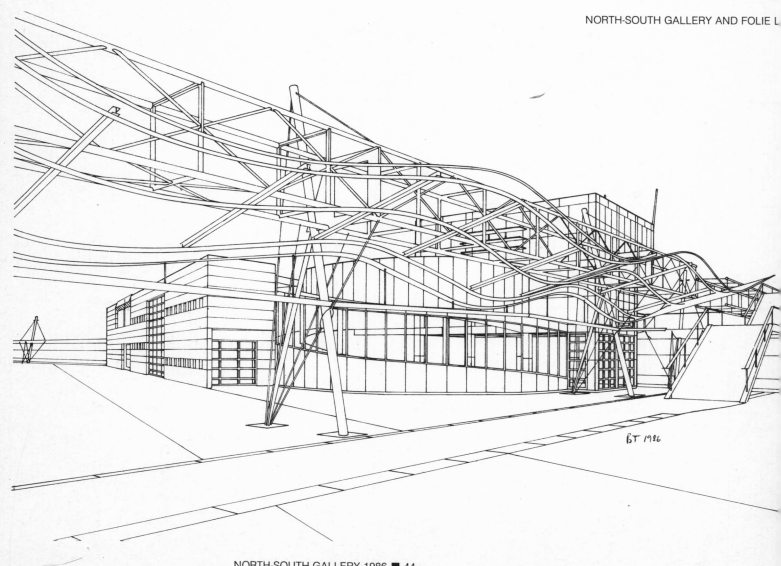

BT 1986

RTH-SOUTH GALLERY AND FOLIE L6   NORTH-SOUTH GALLERY AND FOLIE L7

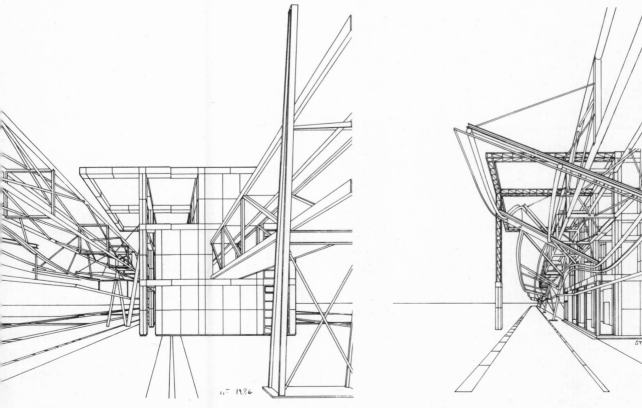

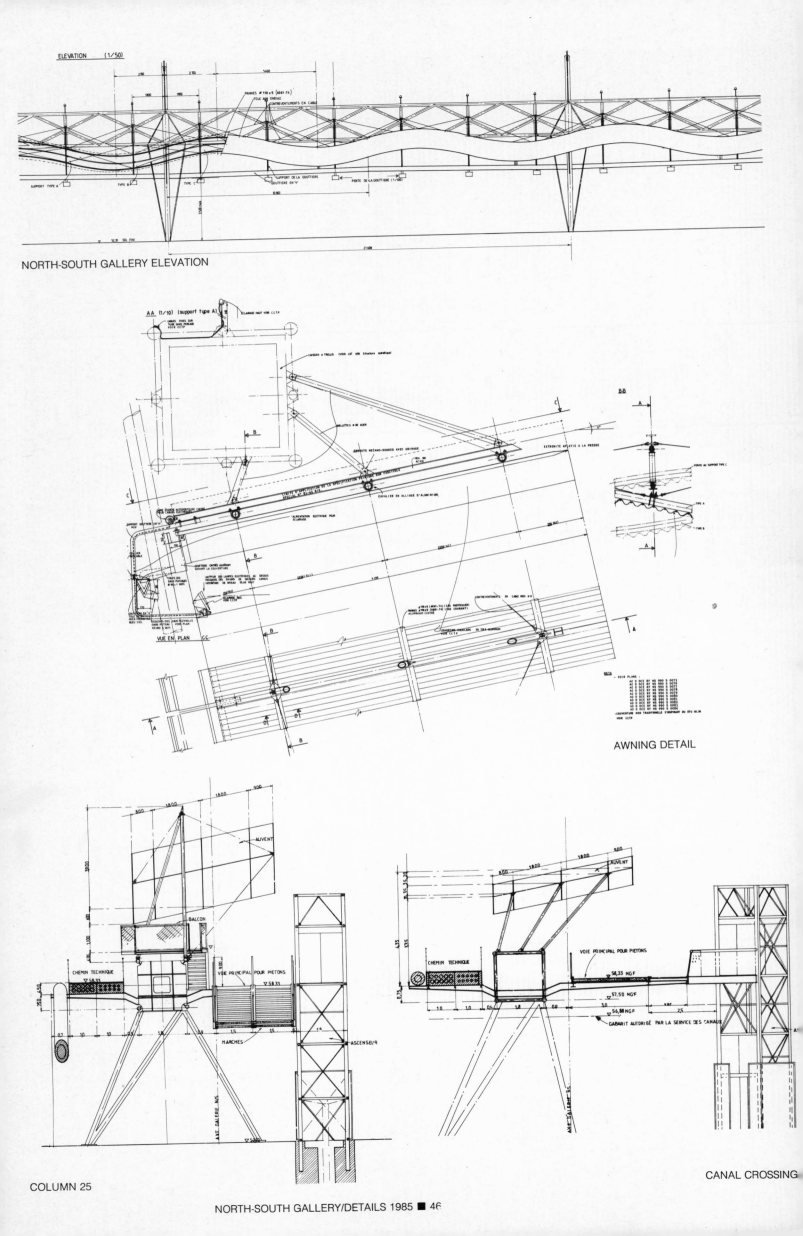

NORTH-SOUTH GALLERY ELEVATION

AWNING DETAIL

COLUMN 25

CANAL CROSSING

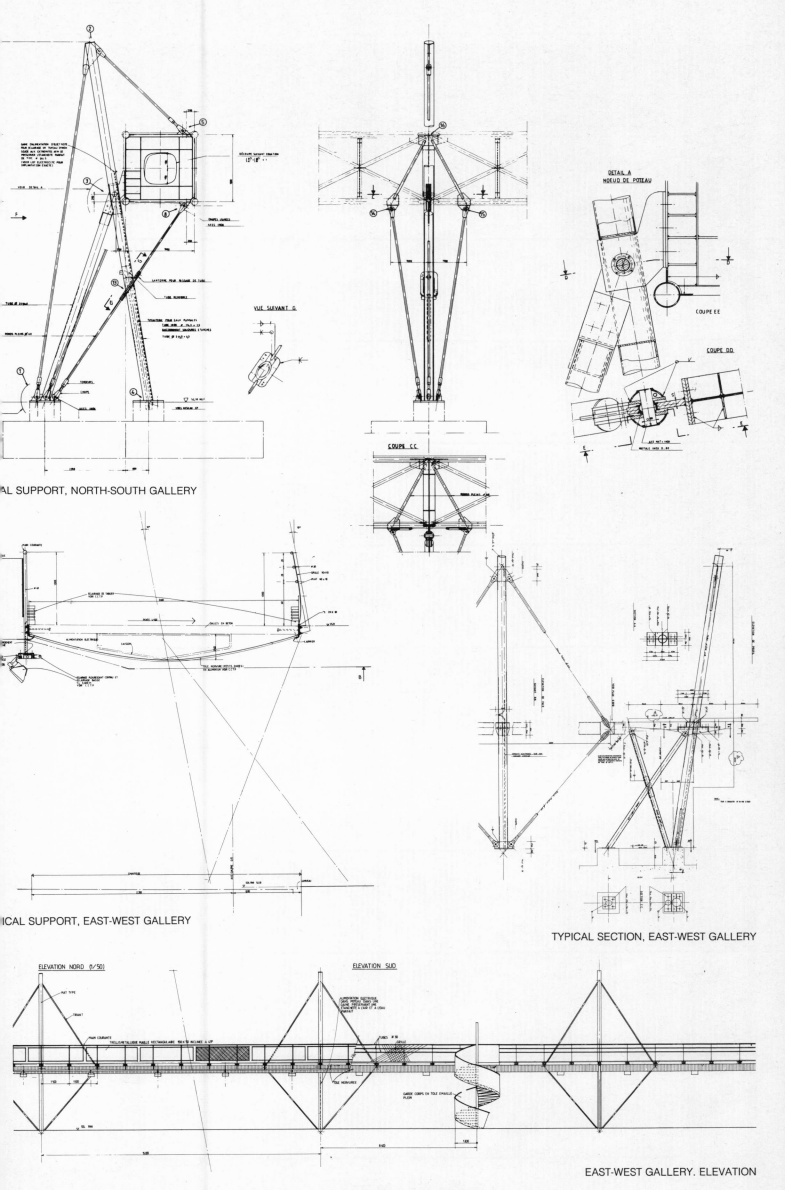

AL SUPPORT, NORTH-SOUTH GALLERY

VUE SUIVANT G

DETAIL A
NOEUD DE POTEAU

COUPE EE

COUPE DD

COUPE CC

ICAL SUPPORT, EAST-WEST GALLERY

TYPICAL SECTION, EAST-WEST GALLERY

ELEVATION NORD (1/50)

ELEVATION SUD

EAST-WEST GALLERY. ELEVATION

BRIDGE OVER THE CANAL DE L'OURCQ

GALLERY AND FOLIE

DETAIL ∨

NORTH - SOUTH GALLERY, MODELS 1986 ■ 48

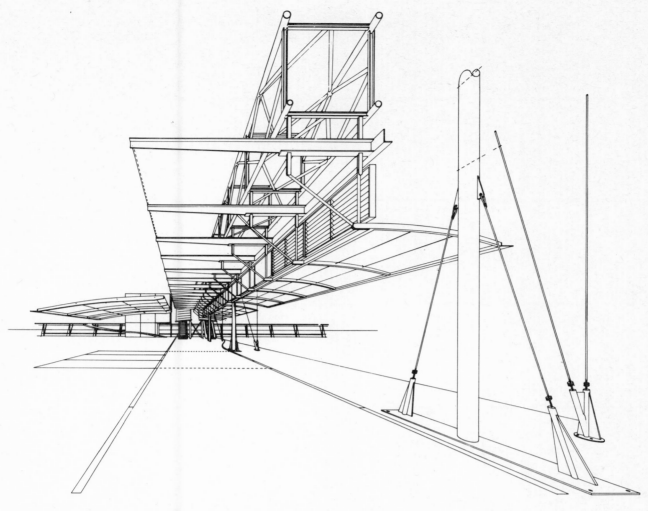

NORTH-SOUTH GALLERY, EARLY PROJECT 1984

P R O G R A M   A N D   D I S T A N C I A T I O N

At La Villette (or anywhere else, for that matter) there is no longer any relationship possible between architecture and program, architecture and meaning. It has been suggested, in discussing La Villette, that architecture must produce a distance between itself and the program it fulfills. This is comparable to the effect of distanciation first elaborated in the performing arts as the principle of non-identity between actor and character. In the same way, it could be said that *there must be no identification* between architecture and program: a bank must not look like a bank, nor an opera house like an opera house, nor a park like a park. This distanciation can be produced either through calculated shifts in programmatic expectations, or through the use of some mediating agent—an abstract parameter that acts as a distancing agent between the built realm and the user's demands (at La Villette, this agent was the grid of *Folies*).

The concept of program, however, remains increasingly important. By no means should it be eliminated (a "pure" architecture) or re-injected at the end of the development of a "pure" architectonic elaboration. The program plays the same role as narrative in other domains: it can and must be reinterpreted, rewritten, deconstructed by the architect. La Villette, in this sense, is dys-narrative or dys-programmatic: the programmatic content is filled with calculated distortions and interruptions, making for a city fragment in which each image, each event strives towards its very concept.

Gardens have had a strange fate. Their history has almost always anticipated the history of cities. The orchard grid of man's earliest agricultural achievements preceded the layout of the first military cities. The perspectives, diagonals and archetypal schemes of the Renaissance Gardens were applied to Squares, Colonnades and design of Renaissance cities. Similarly, the Romantic picturesque parks of English empiricism preempted the Crescents, Arcades and rich urban design tradition of nineteenth century England.

Built exclusively for delight, gardens are like the earliest experiments in that part of architecture that is so difficult to express with words or drawings: pleasure and eroticism. Whether "romantic" or "classic," gardens merge the sensual pleasure of space with the pleasure of reason, in a most useless manner.

Excerpt from "The Pleasure of Architecture," Bernard Tschumi, in *Architectural Design*, London 3/1977.

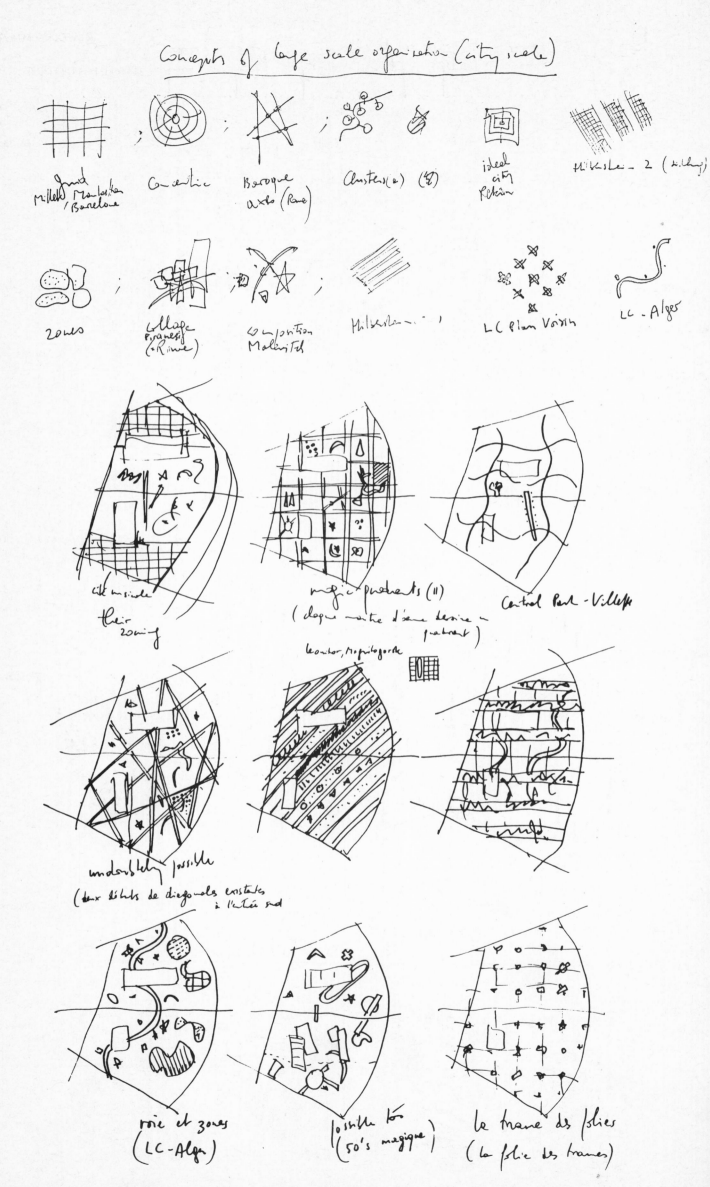

Concepts of large scale organization (city scale)

Milled Manhattan / Barcelona ; Concentric ; Baroque axes (Rome) ; Clusters (a) (b) ; Ideal city Relation ; Hilberseimer - 2 (Walling)

Zones ; Collage Piranesi (*Rome) ; Composition Modernist ; Hilberseimer - 1 ; LC Plan Voisin ; LC - Alger

cité verticale / their zoning

magic patterns (II) (chaque partie d'une dessin à patterns)

Leonidov, Magnitogorsk

Central Park - Villette

undoubtedly possible (deux débuts de diagonales existantes à l'entrée sud

voie et zones (LC - Alger)

possible too (50's magique)

le trame des folies (la folie des trames)

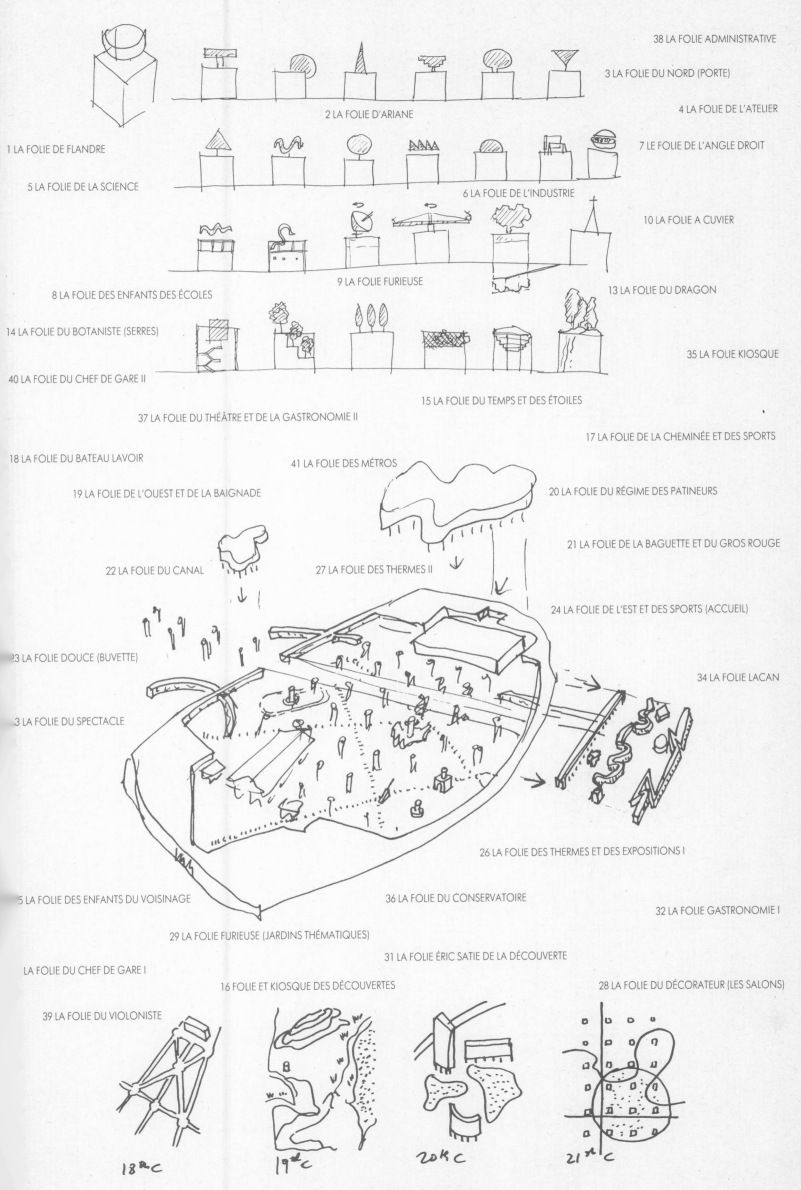

38 LA FOLIE ADMINISTRATIVE

3 LA FOLIE DU NORD (PORTE)

4 LA FOLIE DE L'ATELIER

2 LA FOLIE D'ARIANE

1 LA FOLIE DE FLANDRE

7 LE FOLIE DE L'ANGLE DROIT

5 LA FOLIE DE LA SCIENCE

6 LA FOLIE DE L'INDUSTRIE

10 LA FOLIE A CUVIER

8 LA FOLIE DES ENFANTS DES ÉCOLES

9 LA FOLIE FURIEUSE

13 LA FOLIE DU DRAGON

14 LA FOLIE DU BOTANISTE (SERRES)

35 LA FOLIE KIOSQUE

40 LA FOLIE DU CHEF DE GARE II

15 LA FOLIE DU TEMPS ET DES ÉTOILES

37 LA FOLIE DU THÉÂTRE ET DE LA GASTRONOMIE II

17 LA FOLIE DE LA CHEMINÉE ET DES SPORTS

18 LA FOLIE DU BATEAU LAVOIR

41 LA FOLIE DES MÉTROS

19 LA FOLIE DE L'OUEST ET DE LA BAIGNADE

20 LA FOLIE DU RÉGIME DES PATINEURS

21 LA FOLIE DE LA BAGUETTE ET DU GROS ROUGE

22 LA FOLIE DU CANAL

27 LA FOLIE DES THERMES II

24 LA FOLIE DE L'EST ET DES SPORTS (ACCUEIL)

23 LA FOLIE DOUCE (BUVETTE)

34 LA FOLIE LACAN

3 LA FOLIE DU SPECTACLE

26 LA FOLIE DES THERMES ET DES EXPOSITIONS I

5 LA FOLIE DES ENFANTS DU VOISINAGE

36 LA FOLIE DU CONSERVATOIRE

32 LA FOLIE GASTRONOMIE I

29 LA FOLIE FURIEUSE (JARDINS THÉMATIQUES)

31 LA FOLIE ÉRIC SATIE DE LA DÉCOUVERTE

LA FOLIE DU CHEF DE GARE I

28 LA FOLIE DU DÉCORATEUR (LES SALONS)

16 FOLIE ET KIOSQUE DES DÉCOUVERTES

39 LA FOLIE DU VIOLONISTE

18ᵉ C   19ᵉ C   20ᵏ C   21ᵉ C

buis qui fleurit de différents couleurs.

place aux lions

le loup Grande muelle

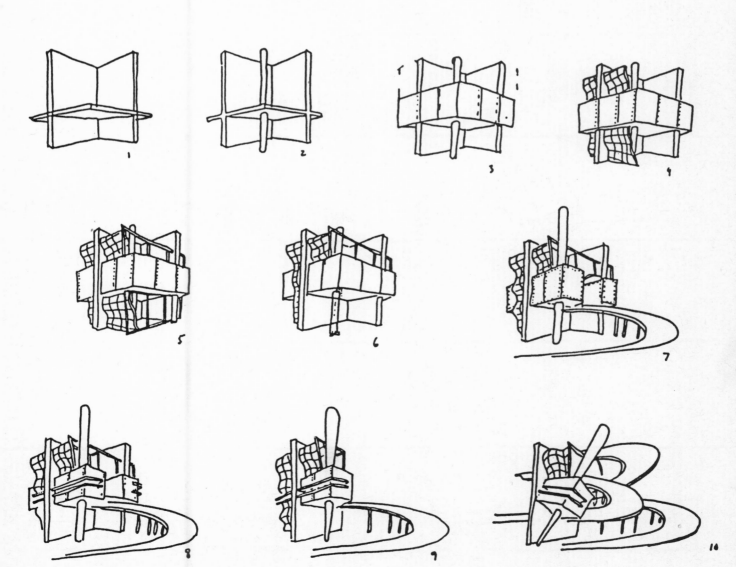

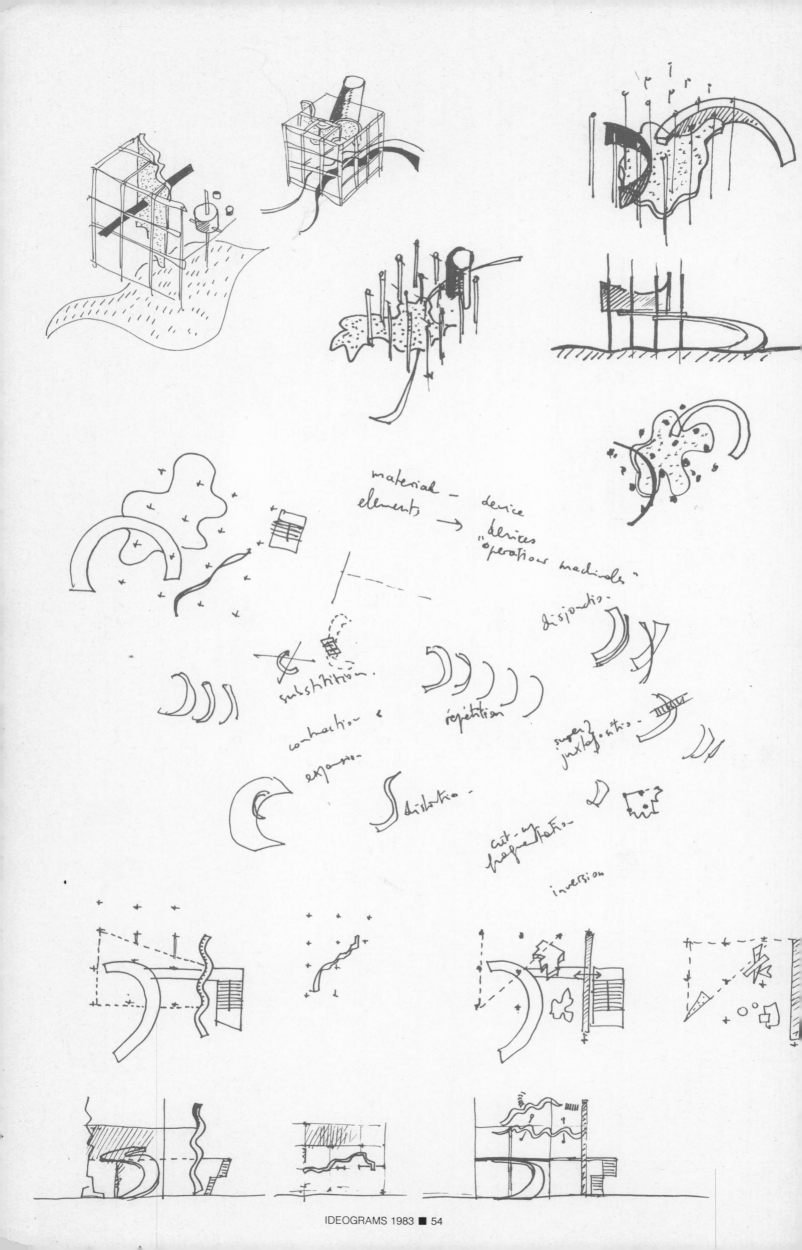

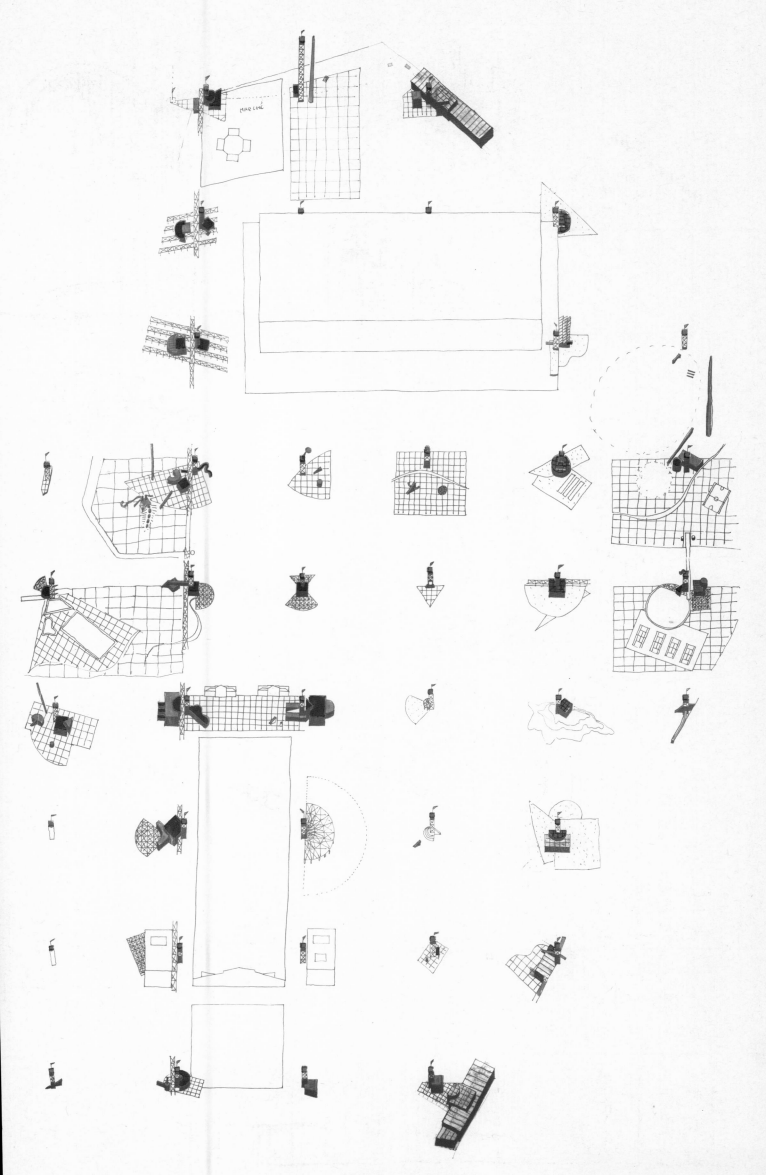

CLIENT BODY
The French Government
The Ministry of Culture
Serge Goldberg
President of the Etablissement Public du Parc de
la Villette
François Barré
Directeur du Parc

ARCHITECTS
International Competition 1982-83
Bernard Tschumi, assisted by Luca Merlini
With Alexandra Villegas, Luca Pagnamenta
And Galen Cranz, Phoebe Cutler
William Wallis, Jon Olsen, Thomas Balsley

Preliminaries and general planning documents
1983-84
Bernard Tschumi, assisted by Colin Fournier
With Luca Merlini, Alexandra Villegas, Neil
Porter, Steve McAdam, Luca Pagnamenta,
Marie-Line Luquet
Jean-Pierre Nourry, Didier Pasquier, Kathryn
Gustafson, Renzo Bader
With Peter Rice (RFR, Structures), Henry Barsley,
SETEC-TP, SETEC-Bâtiment, Commins-BBM,
Kate Linker
And Don Paine, Patrizia Falcone, Patrick
Bouchain, Julia Bourke, Dina Daini, Peter Fleis-
sig, David Kessler, Veronique Metadier, Marina
Merson, Pietr Zaborski, Jon Olsen.

Project and construction 1985
Bernard Tschumi, assisted by Jean-François
Erhel
With Alexandra Villegas, Ursula Kurz
With Luca Merlini, Christian Biecher, Marie-Line
Luquet
With Peter Rice (RFR, Bridge and Galleries Struc-
tures), Hugh Dutton, Henry Bardsley, Nadia Petit,
Bernard Vaudeville
With SETEC-Bâtiment, Pierre Robert; SETEC-TP,
François Demouy, Jean-Paul Bonroy
And Jean-Louis Raynaud, Vincent Polsinelli,
Patrick Winters, Mitsugu Osakawa, George Ka-
todrytis, Rawia Muderris.
Modelmaker: Jacques Fiore

Chronology of research preliminary to the la Villette project:
1976 Joyce's Garden: theoretical project based
on James Joyce's Finnegans Wake. Exhibited at
Centre Pompidou, Paris, 1980.
1976-81 The Manhattan Transcripts: book introducing sequential, superimposition and deconstruction devices. (Academy Editions/St. Martin's
Press, London, New York, 1981).
1979-81 20th Century Follies: experimental constructions of a polemical and ephemeral nature
built in New York, London and Middleburg, Hol-
land.
1985-86 La Case Vide: twenty plates exploring
future conceptual transformations and disloca-
tions of the la Villette project. With an essay on
Bernard Tschumi by Jacques Derrida, an introduction by Anthony Vidler and an interview with
Alvin Boyarsky. (Bernard Tschumi, Folio VIII,
Architectural Association, London, 1986).

BIBLIOGRAPHY (Excerpts)
"La Villette: An Urban Park for the 21st Cen-
tury," International Architect, 1/83.
"Architecture, Limites at Programmes," Art Press,
H.S. no. 2/83.
"Il Parco delle 'Folies' di Tschumi," Casabella,
6/83.
"Concours International pour le Parc de la Vil-
lette," Architecture d'Aujourd'hui no. 227, 6/83.
"Le footballeur patine sur le Champ de Bataille,"
by Kenneth Frampton, Architecture d'Aujourd'hui,
no. 228, 9/83.
"Illustrated Index," AA Files, London, 6/83.
"Interview," Crée no. 197, Paris, 10/83.
"Parc de la Villette," Architectural Review no.
1040, London, 10/83.
"Séquences," Princeton Journal, Vol. 1, Ritual,
1983.
"Bernard Tschumi et les 'Folies' de la Villette,"
Le Monde Dimanche, Paris, 11/20/83.
"Superpositions et Communs Dénominateurs"
(with Colin Fournier), Urbanisme no. 203, Paris,
8/84.
"Madness and the Combinative," Precis, Colum-
bia University, New York, Fall 1984.
"Séquences," in Vivre l'Architecture—Revue
Autrement, Paris, 1984.
"A Paris for the 21st Century," (by Hélène
Lipstadt), Art in America, New York, 11/84.
"Work-in Progress," in l'Invention du Parc, Edi-
tions Graphite, Paris, 1984.
"Bernard Tschumi, le Parc de la Villette," AMC,
12/84.
"Progressive Architecture Awards," Progressive
Architecture, 1/85.
"Close to the madding crowd," by Brian Hatton,
Building Design, London, 5/17/85.
"Close to the madding crowd," by Brian Hatton,
Architectures, New York, Summer 1985.
"A New Modernism," Paul Goldberger, The New
York Times, 11/24/85.
"Landscape and Architecture," Architectural
Review no. 1063, London, 9/85.
"Parc de la Villette," Crée no. 209, Paris, 1/86.
"Séquence 6, Profession Cinéaste" by Claude
Eveno, in "Architecture: récits, figures, fictions,"
Cahiers du CCI, Centre Georges Pompidou,
Paris, 1986.
"La Case Vide," Folio VIII, Architectural Associa-
tion, (textes of Jacques Derrida, Anthony Vidler,
Alvin Boyarsky) London, 1986.
"Art on Location," Artforum, New York, 4/86.
"Point de Folie —Maintenant l'Architecture," by
Jacques Derrida in AA Files no. 12, London,
1986.
"Tschumi—les stries du Parc," Urbanisme no.
215, Paris, 9/86.
"Parco spectacolare di Parigi," Arca no. 1,
Milano, 11/86.
"Parc-Ville Villette," Vaisseau de Pierres, Ed.
Champ Vallon, 1987.
"Architecture et Paysage, Bernard Tschumi,"
Techniques et Architecture, March, 1987.
"Disjunctions, Bernard Tschumi," Perspecta 23,
Yale Architecture Journal, New Haven, 1986.
"The Point of No-Return," Daralice D. Boles, Pro-
gressive Architecture, July 1987.
Les Travaux de Bernard Tschumi, AMC, Paris,
October 1987.

BERNARD TSCHUMI

Architect. Lives New York and Paris. Studied
ETH (Federal Institute of Technology), Zurich.
Taught at the Architectural Association, London,
1970-79; Institute for Architecture and Urban Stu-
dies, New York, 1976; Princeton University, 1976
and 1980; Visiting Professor, Cooper Union
School of Architecture, New York, 1980-83. Lec-
tured extensively throughout United States and
Europe. Exhibited New York, London, Paris,
Copenhagen, Madrid, Kassel, Berlin, Athens,
Moscow, Seoul, Lisbon, Los Angeles and Tokyo.
His critical writings have been published in
numerous architecture and art magazines including Architectural Design, Oppositions, A+U,
Precis, Perspecta, and Artforum.
Prizewinner in many international competitions,
including Parc de la Villette, 1983 (first prize); La
Defense, Paris, 1983 (Award); Tokyo Opera
House, 1986 (Second Prize); also winner of Pro-
gressive Architecture Award, 1985 for Parc de la
Villette.
The first phase of the Parc de la Villette, for which
he is Chief Architect and main designer, will be
completed in 1987. This phase includes fourteen
folies, part of the covered Galleries, the bridge,
and part of the "Cinematic Promenade."

PRINCETON ARCHITECTURAL
PRESS
2 Research Way
Forrestal Center
Princeton, NJ 08540
(609) 987-2424

Design Concept:
Bernard Tschumi, assisted by
Christian Biecher

Design:
Renate Fox and Hubert Tonka

Photography Credits:
Bernard Tschumi, 19,28-29,48
François-X. Bouchart, 48
LART, 20,21,30,31,33-39,42-47

Typography:
M. Dawson, E. Short, A. Urban
Photogravure:
Ernio/Azer (Spain/France)
Vercingétorix-photogravure(France)
SRG (France)

Paper text and cover:
Fedrigoni (Italy)
Printing and Binding:
Néo-Typo (France)

First published 1987 in France
in the series

LIEUX D'ARCHITECTURES
edited by Hubert Tonka
and published by

CHAMP VALLON
01420 SEYSSEL France

© 1987 Bernard Tschumi
ISBN 0-910413-37-1